Still Standing

By

Joanne Maree Duggan

TO MY CHILDREN

I know there were times my love didn't look the way it felt,
for that I am sorry.
But you were never the reason for my hard days.
You are the reason I survived them.
You are my greatest gift, and my deepest joy.

ACKNOWLEDGEMENT

I would like to thank Oliver Brooks for his patience and guidance in helping me put my story to paper.

To Nat, my lifelong friend, whose friendship has been a source of strength and joy. I cherish you and our friendship. It means so much to know you always had my back with no judgement.

Music feeds our soul. How true that was for me with my P!NK music. Thank you for the valuable role your music played in my life. Your songs have made a positive impact on my life.

I would like to thank my son James for telling me to go for it. This is another reason I have told my story.

I would like to thank Karen for her support while I put my story to paper.

Nat, My Lifelong Friend

TABLE OF CONTENT

PREFACE

I used to believe that silence kept you safe. If you didn't talk about the hard things, maybe they'd lose their power. Maybe the past would stay buried where it belonged. But silence doesn't heal; it festers. It turns into tension in your shoulders, anxiety in your chest, and stories that keep repeating themselves in your life until you finally face them. That's why I'm here, telling mine.

This isn't a story of perfection, nor is it a story written to seek sympathy. It's a story of survival, awareness, and, ultimately, growth. I grew up in a home that was never whole, surrounded by people who loved in ways they didn't know how to express. It took me years to understand that love and pain can exist in the same room, that someone can care deeply for you and still hurt you because they're fighting battles you can't see.

When I began reflecting on my childhood, I didn't expect it to lead to a book. It started as journal entries, fragments of memory, observations about the patterns I saw in my own life, and questions I didn't know how to answer. The more I wrote, the clearer one truth became: my story wasn't just mine. It echoed in the experiences of countless others who grew up in homes shaped by separation, conflict, and silence.

Why I'm Sharing My Story

I'm sharing my story because healing doesn't happen in isolation. For too long, society has taught us to hide our pain, to package our struggles neatly and smile through the cracks. But the truth is, what we suppress doesn't disappear; it transforms into the patterns that shape our relationships, our parenting, our confidence, and our sense of self.

I want to break that cycle, not just for myself but for anyone who has ever felt unseen or unheard in their own home. If even one person reads these pages and feels less alone, then the vulnerability of sharing this will have been worth it. There's a tendency to downplay emotional wounds when they don't leave visible scars.

People say things like "You were just a kid" or "That was a long time ago." But emotional neglect, instability, and fear leave impressions that last far beyond childhood. Studies by the National Institute of Mental Health have shown that early exposure to family conflict and emotional inconsistency can alter a child's brain development, particularly in areas linked to stress response and emotional regulation. Those findings helped me understand something profound: trauma isn't always loud. Sometimes, it's the quiet absence of safety that hurts the most.

When I began connecting those insights to my own memories, everything started to make sense. My perfectionism, my fear of confrontation, my tendency to over- explain, these weren't random personality quirks. They were adaptations. They were the ways a child learned to survive in a home where peace felt temporary. Realising that was both painful and liberating.

Sharing this story is my way of giving shape to that understanding. It's a reminder that healing is not about rewriting the past but about reclaiming your power in the present. It's about saying, "This happened, but it no longer defines me."

Breaking the Silence

For years, I carried my childhood like a secret I couldn't speak aloud. I thought if I told the truth about what I'd seen or felt, it would make people uncomfortable, or worse, make them think less of me or my family. But shame only grows in darkness. Once you start talking, the power it holds begins to fade.

There's a quote by Dr. Brené Brown that changed the way I looked at vulnerability: "Owning our story and loving ourselves through that process is the bravest thing that we'll ever do." She's right. It takes courage to face your own reflection without filters, to acknowledge the ways you've been shaped by pain and still choose compassion over bitterness. Writing this book has been an act of courage for me.

I want to invite readers into that same space of honesty. Maybe you didn't grow up in a broken home, but you've felt broken in other ways, by rejection, by loss, by unmet expectations. Maybe you've carried secrets or fears you thought no one would understand. This story isn't about blame; it's about connection. Because at the heart of every human experience lies the desire to be seen and understood.

When I think back to my younger self, I see a child who tried so hard to be good enough that no one would leave again. I see someone who mistook control for safety and silence for strength. Those survival patterns worked for a while, but they came at a cost. Like many adults who grew up in dysfunction, I learned that self-reliance can become a shield and a prison. Breaking that pattern meant learning to trust again, to ask for help, and to believe that I was worthy of peace, not just endurance.

Therapists often talk about the difference between surviving and thriving. Surviving means adapting to dysfunction; thriving means transforming beyond it. That transformation doesn't happen overnight. It's a long, messy process that involves forgiveness, not necessarily of others first, but of yourself. It's the realisation that you did the best you could with what you had, and that even the versions of you who made mistakes were trying to find safety.

Finding Purpose Through Pain

When I first began writing, I didn't know where it would lead. What I found was that storytelling itself became a form of therapy. Studies on expressive writing, such as those by psychologist James Pennebaker, show that putting emotions into words helps reduce stress, improve emotional clarity, and increase a sense of control. I didn't know the science at the time; I just knew that the more I wrote, the lighter I felt.

That's the hidden power of sharing your truth. It not only frees you but invites others to free themselves. When we name our pain, we stop it from silently shaping our future. When we speak our truth, we break the generational patterns that thrive in secrecy. I think that's what healing really is: the decision to no longer carry what was never yours to hold.

This book isn't about casting judgment on anyone from my past. My parents, like so many others, were products of their own unhealed stories. Understanding that doesn't excuse what happened, but it allows me to see them through the lens of compassion instead of resentment. We can't change the people who hurt us, but we can change what we carry forward from them.

To the Reader

If you've picked up this book, I want to thank you for being willing to step into these pages with an open heart. Some parts may mirror your own experiences; others may help you understand someone you love a little better. My hope is that as you read, you'll feel encouraged to look at your own story, not with shame or regret, but with curiosity and gentleness.

We live in a world that glorifies strength but misunderstands what it really means. Real strength isn't about being untouched by pain. It's about facing it, learning from it, and transforming it into empathy. Every scar, whether visible or invisible, tells a story of survival. And every time we share those stories, we remind one another that healing is possible.

This preface is my invitation to break your own silence, to sit with your truth, and to believe that even the most fractured beginnings can lead to beautiful transformations. Because in the end, healing doesn't start with forgetting. It starts with remembering, and then choosing to grow anyway. And so, this is where my story begins. Not with perfection or resolution, but with honesty. Because sometimes the bravest thing you can do is simply tell the truth about where you've been, and trust that someone, somewhere, needs to hear it too.

CHAPTER 1:
CHILDHOOD SHADOWS

I grew up in a broken home. My mum and dad weren't together. In fact, I can't remember them ever being together. My childhood memories are fragments, quiet corners of rooms, muffled arguments, long silences. The story of their separation has been told to me so many times that it almost feels like a movie I've seen instead of something I lived through. Mum said that one night she left my father, taking me and leaving my older sister behind. She went to my grandmother's house in the middle of the night, carrying me in her arms. Later, when she tried to go back for my sister, my dad was awake. She couldn't take her. She had to walk away.

Even though I was too young to remember, that story became part of my identity. My life began with separation. There was love, and there was loss, both in the same breath. Psychologists say that early separation from a parent can shape the way a child forms attachments later in life. Children who experience parental separation often develop what's called an "anxious attachment style," a constant need for reassurance, a fear of abandonment, and a deep sense that love can disappear without warning.

I didn't need a textbook to tell me that was true. I felt it in the way I clung too tightly to friends, the way I avoided conflict, and the way I flinched when people raised their voices. The emotional blueprint of my childhood was written in invisible ink, but it showed up in every relationship I had afterward.

Mum told the story with guilt in her voice. I think she carried that pain for years, maybe forever. In psychology, that's called intergenerational trauma, when a parent's unresolved grief or shame seeps into the next generation. I didn't inherit money or property; I inherited silence, self- blame, and a deep desire to fix what was broken.

My dad remarried soon after, and Mum moved in with someone new while she was pregnant with my little sister. I became part of two families, belonging fully to neither. Research shows that children who grow up in divided homes often develop strong adaptability skills. They learn to navigate shifting emotional landscapes and different sets of rules, but the cost is identity confusion. You become good at blending in but struggle to know who you really are.

It's a strange thing, growing up split between two worlds. You learn to adapt, to please, to perform. You become the kind of child who tries not to upset anyone because you already know what happens when people stop loving each other. I learned early how to read moods, how to shrink when things got tense, how to make myself small enough to avoid becoming a target. That's the quiet education of children from broken homes. We become emotional chameleons, always adjusting to survive.

I grew up in Mornington, a quiet suburb with tree-lined streets and ocean air that smelled faintly of salt. To anyone passing through, it probably looked like a peaceful, middle- class neighbourhood, a place where kids played cricket in the street, and neighbours chatted over fences. But for me, Mornington was the backdrop for chaos. Behind closed doors, peace was a myth. It was there, in that calm suburb, that I first learned how invisible pain could be.

By the age of ten, Mum was dating a man named Kevin. He was kind, gentle even. He didn't drink or swear, and he treated her with a patience that felt foreign in our house. He'd smile when I came into the room, ask about my day, and listen when I spoke. It was such a small thing, being heard, but it meant everything. For a short while, I felt a glimpse of stability. I remember thinking that maybe we'd finally found someone who wouldn't hurt us, who wouldn't leave. But Mum left him. She always did.

After Kevin came Mervin; if Kevin was calm, Mervin was chaos. He drank, shouted, and carried a kind of bitterness that seeped into the walls. Mum drank too, and together they created storms that shook the house. I learned to recognise the warning signs, the clinking of bottles, the change in tone, the silence before the shouting.

When you grow up like that, you become hyperaware. It's called "hypervigilance" in psychology, a trauma response where your body stays on alert even when there's no immediate threat. For me, it was a way of life. Some nights I'd hide in my room, pressing a pillow over my ears, wishing the shouting would stop. I'd look at the ceiling and imagine what it would be like to live somewhere quiet, somewhere where people spoke softly and smiled easily. I didn't know what normal looked like, but I knew I wanted it.

Growing up in a broken home doesn't just change your childhood; it changes the way you see the world. You start believing that love is unstable, that peace is temporary, that safety is conditional. Researchers say children from high-conflict families often develop heightened anxiety and low self-esteem. I didn't have those words back then, but I felt them every day. I felt them in the way my stomach knotted when the phone rang late at night. I felt them in the way I flinched when someone raised their voice, even if it wasn't in anger.

Over time, I began to notice that my nervous system never rested. I'd stay tense, waiting for the next loud word or slammed door. Years later, I'd learn that this was my body's way of protecting me, keeping me safe by keeping me ready. But that constant readiness comes with a cost: exhaustion, mistrust, and the inability to truly relax. It takes conscious effort, therapy, and patience to unlearn it.

In self-help literature, this process is often called reparenting yourself, learning to give your adult self the safety and love your child self never received. It begins with awareness, realising that your reactions aren't flaws but survival strategies. When I finally learned that, it shifted something deep inside me. Instead of blaming myself for being "too sensitive," I began to understand that my sensitivity was actually wisdom, the body's memory of danger, trying to protect me from being hurt again.

If I could offer advice to anyone growing up in a home like that, it would be this: don't mistake chaos for normality. Just because you were raised in turbulence doesn't mean peace is foreign to you; it just means you'll have to learn it later. Healing begins with permission to feel safe again, one breath, one boundary, one gentle moment at a time.

Looking back, Kevin represented what safety might have looked like. Mervin and the others showed what I never wanted to repeat. And between those extremes, I began to form my own understanding of love, not as something that arrives to rescue you, but as something you cultivate from within.

There were moments of light, too, small flickers that kept me going. I had friends at school who came from homes that seemed happy and steady. I watched the way their parents interacted, small gestures of affection, laughter over dinner, and I tried to understand how that kind of love worked. Part of me felt jealous; another part felt inspired. I promised myself that one day, if I ever had a family of my own, I'd make it different.

Still, I couldn't escape the loneliness. Living between two families made me feel like a visitor in both. At Dad's, I was the child of his past life, a reminder of something that didn't work out.

At Mum's, I was her companion in survival. I became her little helper, her confidante, sometimes even her caretaker when the nights ran long. Children shouldn't have to carry adult burdens, but many of us do. We learn to hold our families together with silence.

What I later learned is that this kind of role reversal, when a child becomes emotionally responsible for a parent, is known as parentification. Psychologists describe it as one of the most common but least discussed forms of emotional neglect. It shapes how a person sees relationships for the rest of their life. You grow up believing your worth is tied to how much you can help or fix others. It took me years to realise that love doesn't have to be earned through caretaking; it can simply be received.

Mervin didn't stay long, but his presence left its mark. I remember the way he'd slam doors and the heavy smell of alcohol that lingered in the air. Mum's drinking worsened after he left. She tried to find comfort in the bottle, but it only deepened the void. I learned early that addiction doesn't start as destruction; it starts as escape. People drink to forget, to numb, to avoid feeling what they can't face. But the things you try to drown always float back up.

In my adult years, I've read studies showing how children of addicted parents often internalise the chaos. They may become overachievers, trying to control what they couldn't as kids, or they might struggle with trust and emotional regulation. Knowing this doesn't erase the pain, but it offers understanding, and understanding is the first step to healing.

If I could speak to that younger version of myself, I'd tell them it wasn't their fault. I'd tell them that survival is not the same as living, and that their empathy, though born from hardship, would one day become their greatest strength.

For anyone who's lived through something similar, it helps to remember that your story doesn't end where it began. The patterns we inherit don't have to define the lives we build. Healing is often about rewriting what love, safety, and connection mean to you. And sometimes, it starts simply by saying, "I deserve peace."

In those years, I began to understand fear in a way most children never should. Fear wasn't just about being scared; it was about anticipation. It was about knowing something bad might happen, but not knowing when. It was the tension of waiting for the next argument, the next slammed door, the next tearful apology that never changed anything. Fear, for me, was both a feeling and a rhythm. It lived in the pauses between words, in the echo of footsteps down the hallway. I learned to read moods the way others read books, studying facial expressions, tones, and movements to predict what was coming next.

As I grew older, I realised that my story wasn't unique. Millions of children grow up in homes fractured by separation, addiction, and conflict. Research from the American Psychological Association confirms that children from high-conflict families are more likely to experience anxiety, depression, and trust issues well into adulthood. But numbers can't capture the lived experience, the way it feels to sit quietly in a corner, counting seconds between raised voices, or how your heart races at the sound of breaking glass. The damage of instability isn't just emotional; it rewires your body to live in survival mode.

Trauma researchers like Dr. Bessel van der Kolk explain that chronic stress during childhood can alter the brain's threat-detection systems, leaving individuals "stuck" in patterns of alertness long after danger has passed. I didn't have those words back then, but my body knew. Even years later, loud noises or sudden anger could trigger that same pulse of fear, as if I were still that small child trying to make herself invisible.

Yet, within that fear, something else quietly grew: resilience. Children who endure early instability often develop extraordinary coping mechanisms such as adaptability, empathy, and intuition. Those traits can become superpowers when healed, but burdens when left unaddressed. Healing, I've come to understand, isn't about forgetting the fear. It's about teaching your nervous system that the war is over.

When I look back now, I see how those early experiences shaped the person I became. They taught me resilience, yes, but also fear. They made me empathetic to others' pain but cautious about their love. Healing, I've learned, doesn't mean erasing the past; it means reclaiming your story from it. It's about acknowledging what happened, understanding how it shaped you, and consciously choosing to build something better.

For anyone walking a similar path, the first step toward healing is awareness. When we recognise the patterns born in childhood, people-pleasing, fear of abandonment, and self-blame, we can start to interrupt them. We can learn that safety is not something to chase; it's something we can create. And sometimes, that creation begins in the quiet act of telling your truth.

If there's one lesson I've taken from that time, it's that children are remarkably adaptive. We find ways to survive even when the world around us feels unstable. Psychologists call this "adaptive functioning," the ability to adjust emotionally and behaviourally to difficult environments. For children in chaotic homes, it often means learning to manage emotions alone, reading danger cues early, and finding small sources of comfort where none seem to exist. But survival isn't the same as healing. Survival keeps you alive; healing helps you live. Healing takes awareness, honesty, and time. It requires revisiting the places you've buried, not to live there again, but to finally leave them behind.

Growing up in Mornington, surrounded by dysfunction, I learned to be both strong and small, to stand tall in public and shrink in private. I became the peacemaker, the responsible one, the quiet observer. Many children from broken homes develop what family therapists call a "parentified role," where they become caretakers far too early. I tried to be good enough that no one would leave again. I helped, listened, cleaned, stayed quiet, and tried to fix what I never broke. But deep down, I still felt that hollow space where security should have been.

That emptiness followed me into adolescence. I excelled at keeping things together on the outside, but inside, I was constantly anticipating collapse. Research on attachment theory by Dr. Mary Ainsworth and later by Dr. Sue Johnson suggests that early relational instability often leads to anxious or avoidant attachment styles in adulthood, patterns where we either cling to love or push it away, terrified of both losing and needing it. I could see myself in that. I loved deeply but feared it too, because love in my experience had always come with conditions or consequences.

When I talk to others who grew up in similar circumstances, I often remind them: it's okay to grieve the childhood you didn't get. Many of us grow up too fast, taking on roles that weren't meant for us. We become adults who know how to care for others but not ourselves. Grief is not self- pity; it's acknowledgment. It's giving yourself permission to feel sadness for the stability, affection, and innocence you were denied. Without acknowledgment, we end up repeating the same emotional patterns, chasing healing through achievement or relationships that can never quite fill the void.

Breaking that cycle starts with compassion, first for the people who hurt you, and then for yourself. That doesn't mean excusing harmful behaviour. It means understanding that most pain is recycled; wounded people often wound others.

Compassion helps you put down the burden of resentment so you can carry something lighter, wisdom.

As I write this now, I can see how every piece of my story connects. The night my mother left my father. The years of instability. The men who came and went. The loneliness followed me like a shadow. It all became part of my foundation, not to define me, but to teach me what I needed to unlearn. Healing isn't linear; it's a spiral. You revisit the same lessons at deeper levels until you can see them with clarity instead of pain.

For anyone reading this who came from a similar place, know this: your past may explain you, but it doesn't have to control you. You can choose to build differently. You can choose peace, even if you were raised in chaos. You can choose to love, even if love once hurt you. You can choose to rest, even if you were taught to always be on guard. Most importantly, you can choose to heal, not perfectly, not all at once, but with intention and patience.

That's the first truth I learned from my childhood shadows: even in the darkest home, a small light survives. And sometimes, surviving is the first act of courage. Over time, survival can grow into strength, and strength into wisdom. And maybe, just maybe, the greatest redemption of all is learning to become the safe place you never had.

CHAPTER 2:
MERVIN ENTERS OUR LIVES

Life before Mervin felt ordinary in its monotony, a rhythm my sister and I had learned to navigate. My mother never worked, so her days were long and uneventful, filled with routines that left little room for warmth or connection. She was often distant, preoccupied with maintaining the house or managing her own frustrations. There was no tenderness in her eyes, just the persistent weight of obligation and survival.

Mervin came into our lives through his sister. She spoke highly of him, describing him as responsible, trustworthy, and someone children could be around. My mother, accustomed to handling everything alone, seemed drawn to the idea of someone steady nearby. Mervin appeared polite and friendly, the sort of adult whose presence could be trusted—or so it seemed. For a while, he was just another adult in the house, someone who helped in small ways when my mother needed relief.

At first, nothing felt unusual. Mervin visited occasionally, careful in his words, courteous in his gestures. My mother responded with a rare spark of interest when he was around, though it was more a relief at having company than genuine affection. She would adjust her appearance before his visits, a perfunctory attention to detail, and leave with a soft smile, but it was not warmth we recognised. The house would feel emptier after she left, yet her distance was consistent, unaffected by his presence.

During those visits, my sister and I were often left with babysitters, usually neighbours or family friends. Evenings passed with us in pajamas, watching television until bedtime. Mervin would sit with us sometimes, asking superficial questions about school, occasionally bringing small gifts. At that age, I saw him as just another adult, someone whose moods were unpredictable, but nothing about him seemed threatening.

The change was gradual, subtle at first. When my younger sister was asleep, Mervin's behaviour shifted. Small touches, almost imperceptible, began to happen. I didn't know how to process it. Fear and confusion built inside me, and I stayed silent. Each incident made me feel smaller, trapped in a quiet terror I couldn't articulate. I tried to distract myself, pretend to be asleep, or busy myself with trivial tasks, hoping it would stop. It never did.

Over time, the touches became deliberate, frequent, impossible to ignore. I dreaded Mervin's visits; every step of his approach stirring tension in me. I couldn't tell my sister; she was too young, and I instinctively tried to shield her. My mother remained unaware. She trusted him. She wanted someone dependable in her life. I didn't want to ruin that or risk her anger, so I hid what was happening. The fear weighed on me silently, shaping my days, shrinking the world around me.

Bedtime became a minefield. I curled up tightly, hoping stillness would make me invisible. I whispered to myself that maybe it was my fault, that if I stayed quiet, it might stop. But the reality was relentless. He would put his fingers inside me, threaten me not to tell my mother, and claim that if I spoke, both of us would be in trouble. The room that should have been safe became a cage.

Nearly a year passed in this tension. Each visit intensified the fear. Mervin's manipulation thrived in the gap between a mother who was too distant to notice and children too young to assert themselves. My younger sister's presence offered a fragile shield—I made sure she fell asleep quickly, tried to keep her close, and found excuses to protect her from the reality I faced. I didn't fully recognise the change in myself. I only knew a part of me was shutting down, retreating.

The night that changed everything arrived quietly. Mervin was scheduled to babysit again. I felt a stirring unease I could no longer suppress. My sister played nearby, unaware of the storm I carried inside. When my mother announced her plans to leave, I spoke with a trembling yet determined voice: "I don't want him to babysit tonight."

Her confusion was immediate. She asked why, expecting a simple answer. I tried to explain, but the words were heavy, fragmented, and difficult to articulate. Finally, I said, "I don't feel safe with him." The room froze for a moment. The weight of my statement slowly settled over her. Something in her expression shifted from puzzlement to alarm. She began to connect the subtle unease she may have ignored, the unusual behaviours, the quiet tension in the house. She understood, finally, that Mervin's presence was a danger.

My mother confronted Mervin without delay. At first, he denied everything, insisting nothing improper had occurred. She pressed, refusing intimidation or excuses, demanding truth and accountability. In response, he became verbally abusive, hurling threats and insults. My mother, unwavering, stood firm, her attention entirely on the safety of her children.

The situation required police involvement. Investigations were thorough, methodical, and emotionally taxing. Every detail, every recollection, had to be documented. I remember sitting in the living room during interviews, trying to answer questions without reliving every memory aloud, some of which were too raw to articulate. My mother's resolve guided me through that process. She coordinated with authorities, maintained a protective presence, and ensured our voices mattered.

The months leading to that confrontation now seem surreal. Warning signs had existed, subtle yet undeniable. Children often lack the power to fully articulate threats, especially from trusted adults. Only when I spoke clearly did the truth become undeniable.

Afterward, Mervin was barred from the house. Legal proceedings unfolded, and life gradually shifted toward normalcy. Counselling, supportive conversations, and the reassurance of safety helped me and my sister reclaim our sense of security. Though scars remained, the ordeal instilled lessons about trust, courage, and vigilance.

My mother arranged hospital visits for me. The tests were routine, meant to ensure no lasting physical harm. The details blur now, but the message was clear: my experiences mattered. The adults around me were listening, watching, and taking action.

Over time, fear receded. Mervin never returned. The house felt lighter. We could play, laugh, and move without constant tension. Yet the memories remained, reminders of the fragility of safety and the importance of speaking out. I learned to trust instincts, assert boundaries, and recognise danger—even in the guise of someone trusted.

The chapter with Mervin ended, but the lessons endured. Courage, vigilance, and the presence of someone who believes in you can protect and heal. My mother, flawed and distant as she was, became a figure of protection when it mattered most. She showed that decisiveness and awareness could confront even the most manipulative threats.

That time shaped me profoundly. Fear, courage, and intuition became intertwined. Speaking up changed everything. Trusting myself became vital. Though painful, the experience taught lessons about safety, resilience, and the strength it takes to face wrongdoing.

Mervin is gone. His threat was eliminated. The darkness lifted slowly, replaced by understanding, security, and the knowledge that speaking out can be life-changing.

CHAPTER 3:
SURROUNDED BY ADDICTION

Addiction does not always begin with chaos. It often begins quietly, appearing as a way to unwind or escape. Gradually, it takes over the rhythms of a home. It seeps into conversations, morning routines, even the spaces between people. At first, it seems harmless. Over time, it becomes the centre of everything.

Life in a home with addiction feels like walking on unstable ground. Moments of laughter appear briefly, followed by long stretches of silence or tension. The atmosphere shifts constantly. Small sounds signal either peace or conflict. Children learn to read the air, to anticipate moods, to adjust before words are spoken. Responsibilities meant for adults become obligations for those too young to carry them.

Addiction touches everyone nearby. It shapes thoughts, feelings, and actions. It replaces security with unpredictability. A parent may still love, but that love is clouded by confusion, guilt, or preoccupation. The household moves around addiction as if it were a fragile secret, never to be disturbed. Silence becomes survival. Pretending that all is normal becomes routine.

A child's understanding of the shifts in their world is limited. Warmth can disappear overnight. The person who once read bedtime stories might vanish behind bottles and exhaustion. Children adapt, becoming quiet, careful, and vigilant. That early watchfulness develops strength, but it leaves a deep ache, a sense of responsibility that is not theirs to bear.

Addiction wears many masks. In some homes, it is loud and destructive, full of anger and broken promises. In others, it hides behind normal routines, music, laughter, and half-empty glasses.

It can coexist with affection, yet bury that affection under exhaustion, regret, and absence. It begins as comfort, then erodes into isolation.

I remember mornings clearly, when the scent of wine was part of waking. My mother always said mornings were the hardest, that a small glass helped her take the edge off. Her hands often trembled until that first glass was gone. She poured quietly, sometimes before brushing her hair, and sat at the kitchen table with a cigarette, staring at nothing.

The sound of a cork pulling free became our morning bell. While other children woke to cereal and cartoons, I woke to clinking glass and the soft hum of a record spinning, Fleetwood Mac or Elton John, sunlight cutting through dusty curtains, glinting on empty bottles lining the counter.

When the parties ended, the house fell into silence. That was when my part began. I woke before anyone else, moving quietly through the wreckage. Bottles tipped on their sides, some still sticky with spilt wine. Half-filled glasses floated cigarette butts like boats. I gathered everything into a garbage bag, careful not to disturb Mum. It was a secret duty, one I assumed to keep the house livable.

The adult world made no sense to me. Smells, smoke, perfume, and sounds filled the air, strange and overwhelming. Mum sometimes fell asleep on the couch, still dressed, music playing. I would cover her with a blanket, move bottles off the table, and tuck my sister back into bed. These small acts gave me the illusion of control, the sense that someone had to hold the house together.

Friends, strangers, and acquaintances from work came and went. Faces blurred together in a long night without end. I longed for normalcy, for quiet mornings, for a mother who could smile without the haze of alcohol. TV families seemed to live in worlds I could barely imagine.

As months passed, Mum's drinking deepened. Curtains stayed drawn, the air thick with alcohol and regret. I became adept at pretending all was fine when visitors came. I cleaned obsessively, stacked bottles, and imagined one day the routine would break. I told myself that if the house were spotless, Mum might notice what she was doing to herself and to us. Yet mornings were always the same, wine in her glass, eyes fixed on nothing.

Those years shaped me profoundly. Responsibility arrived too early, silence too easily. I learned that care could coexist with destruction. Children become quiet witnesses to adult chaos, carrying burdens that never belonged to them.

The desire to speak up came sometimes, but words failed me. In our house, silence was protection. As long as no one asked questions, the world continued predictably, even if dysfunction ruled beneath the surface.

Certain smells pull me back even now: cheap red wine, faint cigarette smoke. They remind me of mornings standing in the kitchen, sunlight slicing through dust, hoping the day would be different. It rarely was. Yet hope persisted quietly that somewhere beneath the haze, Mum could have been different, could have chosen another path.

By the mid-1980s, I was in high school. The world outside our house operated on structure: bells, teachers, friends. That order became an escape. At school, I glimpsed what life might have been, a place where parents woke clear- headed, where weekends smelled of breakfast instead of wine.

Returning home, the smell of alcohol was a constant reminder of reality. Wine glasses occupied the counters like furniture, surrounded by plates and cups. I opened windows to push stale air outside, even in winter, frost biting my fingers. I wanted to protect myself from the smells clinging to clothes before stepping outside.

The school offered both respite and awareness. Conversations about families and activities highlighted the contrast. My weekends remained spent cleaning, clearing, and maintaining a fragile semblance of order. I didn't yet know the word addiction, but I recognised its impact: mornings stolen, nights altered, laughter replaced with tension. Mum was simultaneously present and absent.

Walking home through the park, I imagined a sober mother, smiling, laughing in the sunlight. Those images existed only in my mind. The reality at the front door was always the same: wine and smoke. Yet, amidst it all, I persisted. I studied, cleaned, cared for my sister, and held the pieces of our life together. Survival became an unspoken skill, learned in silence.

As I grew older, expression became restrained. I stopped seeking Mum's attention, knowing she had little to give. Loneliness became familiar, a constant companion inside a family. Feeling invisible served as armour, shielding me from disappointment while hiding the need for help. I eventually understood that invisibility was not a reflection of my worth but of the adults' incapacity to see.

Looking back, anger has faded. Sadness remains—for the girl who carried the household while the adults around her faltered. She deserved more than silence. She deserved recognition. That quiet strength, learned through years of chaos, became the foundation for resilience, the ability to navigate life even when those around her could not.

CHAPTER 4:
THE ACCIDENT THAT CHANGED ME

Life can change in a single moment, and sometimes that change comes not from something you did, but from something that was done to you. I remember that morning with the kind of clarity that trauma brings, the way certain details burn themselves into your memory while others blur at the edges. My neighbour and friend, Andrew, and I were trying to find work. We would wake up at seven some mornings to get to the popcorn cart on time, and on this particular day, the streets were quiet, the air cool, and I felt the usual mix of excitement and nervousness that came with an early start. We walked together, joking and laughing, completely unaware that the day would turn into one of the most frightening and painful experiences of my life.

Andrew was playing around with a forklift that day. He liked going up and down on it repeatedly, just testing it for fun, and I was leaning against a wall near some pallets, trying to stay out of the way. I was not worried. We were friends. I trusted him. When he started driving the forklift toward me, I thought it was just a prank, just him trying to scare me a bit. At first, it seemed harmless, the kind of thing teenage boys do without thinking. But the forklift did not stop. The forklift hit me square in the stomach and pinned me against the wall. For several seconds, I could not move. I could not breathe. My body froze. The pain was immediate and enormous; like nothing I had ever felt before. When he finally reversed, I fell to the ground gasping, my chest tight, every breath a fight.

The pain was beyond anything I had words for. My body felt like it no longer belonged to me, like it had been broken into pieces I could not put back together. Waves of sharp, rolling pain moved through me, and I kept passing out. I would wake for a few seconds, confused and terrified, and then lose consciousness again. I have no idea how long I lay there. Time stopped meaning anything. All I knew was pain and fear and the sensation of my body shutting down.

It was around ten in the morning when Andrew's father finally came outside. I do not know what took him so long. I do not know if Andrew told him immediately or if he waited, scared of what he had done. What I do know is this: they did not call an ambulance. They were afraid of getting into trouble, afraid of what might happen if the truth came out. So instead of getting me proper help, they lifted me into the back of the car. I lost control of my bowels. I was lying there in my own mess, in agony, completely helpless. I begged them to ring an ambulance, and they drove me to my mother and told her it was just a small accident. A small accident. As if I had tripped and scraped my knee.

I want to be very clear about something. My mother did not rush to call the ambulance out of love or concern for me. They had to come up with a lie first to protect Andrew and his father. While I lay there in pain, I could hear them talking. They told me I had to tell the ambulance when it arrived, and the hospital, that I had been bucked off my horse. I agreed, and only then did my mother call the ambulance. She took me because it was obvious even to her that something was very wrong, and if she did not take me, people would ask questions. When we arrived at the hospital, her face showed panic, yes, and anger, but not the kind of panic or anger a mother feels when her child is hurt. It was the panic of inconvenience. The anger of disruption. She was annoyed that this had happened, that she now had to deal with it, that her day had been interrupted by my injury.

The doctors rushed me in. They ran tests and X-rays, and the results confirmed what my body had been screaming at me since the moment the forklift hit: I had a broken pelvis. A broken pelvis at twelve years old, an injury that would take months to heal and years to fully recover from. The pain was constant and exhausting. Every movement reminded me of what had been done to me. Every breath was a battle after this. When I was moved from the emergency department and placed on a ward, my mother and Robert were arguing to the point that security asked them both to leave. I was so embarrassed and alone again. Security told them they could come back the next day.

I stayed in the hospital for two weeks. The plaster cast covered me from my ribcage down one leg, and on the other side, it went halfway down, connecting in the middle. I looked like I had been encased in concrete. Moving was almost impossible. Sitting up, even for a few seconds, was exhausting. I had to rely entirely on the nurses for everything. Eating. When I need to come out. Using the bathroom. Turning over in bed. I had never felt so helpless in my life, and I have felt helpless many times since, so that is saying something.

The first time I moved into a wheelchair felt like climbing a mountain. It was awkward, painful, frustrating, and I was terrified I would fall or that the plaster would crack or that something else would go wrong. But I managed it. I sat upright in that wheelchair and rolled myself down the hospital hallway, and even though it was only a few metres, it felt like a victory. A small one, but mine.

Eventually, I was allowed to go home. The plaster was still on. I was still in pain. I still could not walk. Being in the hospital cost my mother bus fares, which she often complained about, and I was taking up her time, which she also wasn't happy about. She wanted me out of the hospital. I want to address something here because it matters, and because the previous version of this chapter got it wrong. My mother did not insist that I go to school because she cared about my education or wanted me to have a normal life. She insisted I go to school because it was easier for her if I was not at home. If I were at school, I would be someone else's problem. If I were at home, she had to look at me, deal with me, acknowledge the fact that I was injured and in pain.

Going to school with a broken pelvis, in a full body cast, was not some inspiring story of perseverance encouraged by a loving parent. It was neglect. It was a twelve-year-old girl being sent out into the world to fend for herself because her mother could not be bothered to care for her properly. The hallways were hard to navigate. The stairs were impossible. The classrooms were full of stares and whispers. Pain and fatigue were my constant companions, and there were days I thought my body would simply give out. But I had no choice. I pushed through because the alternative was staying home with a mother who did not want me there.

Her drinking never stopped. The house remained chaotic. The parties continued. Music and laughter would drift through my room at night, a sharp contrast to my own pain and isolation. I would lie in bed, unable to move, listening to her and her friends getting drunk in the next room, and I would feel so alone it was almost unbearable. I learned to focus on what I could control, which was very little. I learned to keep moving forward while the world around me stayed unpredictable and unsafe.

After several months, the plaster was finally removed. That moment brought relief, yes, but it was only the beginning of a new and different kind of suffering. My legs had grown weak from being immobile for so long. The muscles had wasted away. Walking again was not something that just happened. It required work, pain, and an enormous amount of patience that I was not sure I had.

I started attending the Douglas Rehabilitation Centre three times a week. The sessions were exhausting, both physically and mentally. Each exercise, each step, required concentration and courage. I had to learn to trust my legs again, to rebuild the muscles that had disappeared, to balance carefully so I would not fall. Some days I wanted to quit. Some days, the frustration and fatigue felt like too much. But I kept going, not because I was particularly brave or strong, but because I did not have another option. No one was going to do this for me. No one was going to carry me. If I wanted to walk again, I had to do the work myself.

The rehabilitation went on for years. Even as my body grew stronger, the exercises never became easy. But slowly, I began to regain confidence. I learned to take small steps and to celebrate tiny victories. I learned to appreciate progress even when it was slow and painful. The rehabilitation centre became a place where I could focus on something other than survival. It became a place where I could work toward something, where effort led to results, where I had some control over my own body and my own future.

Going to school during this period was still a challenge. Even after the plaster was removed, I had to navigate hallways and stairs and classrooms while still recovering, while still rebuilding strength, while still in pain most days. My classmates were curious. Some stared. Some whispered. Some offered quiet support, though not many. I learned to adapt. I learned to stay patient with myself. I learned to manage my own expectations and to accept that recovery was not a straight line. Every small success at school, walking from class to class without needing to sit down, sitting through an entire lesson without my body screaming at me, interacting with friends like a normal person, felt like a triumph.

The accident taught me things I wish I had not had to learn so young. It taught me that people will protect themselves before they protect you, even if you are the one who is hurt. It taught me that my mother was not going to save me, not from this and not from anything else. It taught me that my body could be broken and that healing was long and hard and often lonely. It taught me resilience, but not the kind that comes from having support and encouragement. The kind that comes from having no other choice.

I learned to survive physical pain and emotional turbulence. I learned to keep moving forward even when the people around me did not care whether I moved forward or not. The plaster, the wheelchair, the years of rehabilitation, they were not just about healing my body. They were about learning what it meant to persevere when no one was cheering you on. They were about pushing through fear when you are alone with it. They were about reclaiming my life one painful step at a time, knowing that no one was going to hand it back to me.

I survived that accident. I learned to walk again. I went back to school, and I kept going. But I want to be clear about what that survival cost me, and I want to be clear about who was and was not there for me during that time. My mother was not a caring parent during my recovery. She was barely a parent at all. And pretending otherwise does not honour the truth of what I went through. The truth matters. The truth is what I am here to tell.

CHAPTER 5:
FORCED RELATIONSHIPS AND LOST FREEDOM

I was twelve, almost twelve and a half, when my life began to feel like a trap I could not escape. I lived with my mum, her boyfriend Robert, who later became my stepfather, and my little sister. On the surface, it might have looked like a normal family, but inside our home, there was chaos and fear. There were always people in and out of the house, mostly men, some I knew, some I didn't. They came for the weekend parties my mum hosted, starting on Friday and sometimes lasting until Sunday. Alcohol flowed freely, arguments erupted over the smallest things, and I spent most of my days cleaning up spilt drinks and empty cans. I did it to keep my mum happy and protect my sister from the aftermath of the parties.

Panda was one of the first men who truly marked this chapter of my life. He was in his early twenties, always at the parties, always with a drink in his hand. He told my mum he liked me and wanted to take me out. I told her I did not want to go. She insisted, saying it was for her, that I should go out with him to make her life easier. She said he would bring more alcohol, and she would not have to buy it herself. I refused again. She grounded me. I could not go out after school with my friends. I had to go straight home, and if there was takeout for tea, I was not allowed it. My mum's punishments were ways to control me, to make me comply. Eventually, I broke down and agreed to go out with Panda. I wanted her to leave me alone. When I finally said yes, she was pleased, and I was back on her good side.

But the cost of this compliance was my freedom. Panda moved into the house, and I was kicked out of my bedroom to make space for him. Life at my mum's house was ruled by her moods and the constant presence of alcohol. Robert, her boyfriend, would sometimes wet himself on the kitchen or lounge room floor, leaving me to clean it up. I had no choice but to accept this as part of my daily life.

My mum had more male friends than female friends. Some nights she would wake me, not my little sister, to introduce me to her male friends. Some of them were polite, but others paid far too much attention. She would make me sit on Robert's knee or on the knees of her friends. If I refused, she would squeeze my arm and guide me to them. She would tell me to kiss them. I kissed their cheeks because I was too scared to do otherwise. At twelve, I did not understand why my mum made me do this. I just knew I had to comply or face consequences.

Some days were better than others. When I could stay at my grandmother's, I felt normal. Those nights were my only refuge. They were quiet, safe, and full of small joys. My grandmother would drop in on Tuesdays after work, bringing sweets, bananas, and sometimes bread with cheese and bacon on top. We could have a slice while she was there, but once she left, the house returned to being a place for adults. At home, my life revolved around my mum's moods and the expectations she imposed.

Panda's presence made everything harder. My mum instructed me to go with him to pick up money from my grandmother for alcohol. I had to lie, saying it was for school. On the way back, Panda would always stop at the school car park and try to kiss me. I would say no. He would insist, just one kiss, then we could leave. Eventually, I would give in. I obeyed because survival meant compliance. At twelve, my freedom was gone.

School offered only a temporary escape. I rarely brought friends home, embarrassed by what my life had become. My mum warned me that what happened in her house stayed in her house and had nothing to do with anyone else. I learned early that I could trust no one, not even my mum.

Cleaning up after the parties became a daily routine. I wanted to be invisible, to avoid drawing attention, and to survive each day without punishment. It was exhausting and humiliating. My life was not my own. I had very little control over anything, yet I had to navigate this chaos while protecting my sister. She was younger, innocent, and unaware of the dangers surrounding her.

There were moments of small relief. Nights at my grandmother's were precious. They were filled with laughter, comfort, and a sense of security I could not find elsewhere. I treasured these moments, knowing they were temporary. Once I returned home, the weight of fear and obedience came back. The bedroom I had lost to Panda, the smell of alcohol, and the unpredictable mood swings reminded me that my childhood was slipping through my fingers.

My mum's control extended to every aspect of my life. I could not leave the house at will. I could not spend time with friends. Everything revolved around her whims. Meals could be withheld, privileges removed, and my movements restricted. Each day, I had to carefully navigate her moods, the constant presence of alcohol, and the men she brought into the house. My body, my feelings, and my choices were no longer my own.

Every ride with Panda, every stop at the school car park, every insistence on a kiss reminded me of my lack of choice. He was young, older than me, and yet held power over me because of my mum's instructions. Compliance was safety. Obedience was survival. At twelve, I was learning lessons no child should have to learn.

Even in this chaos, I found small ways to reclaim a fragment of control. I would kiss Panda on the cheek instead of the lips. I would move quickly to clean up before anyone noticed. I would hide my emotions, smile when I wanted to cry, and laugh when I wanted to scream. Each small act of autonomy, no matter how minor, became a lifeline.

Fear was constant. I feared my mum, Panda, and the other adults in the house. I feared punishment, ridicule, and the consequences of defiance. My body learned tension, my mind calculated every interaction, and my heart sank under the weight of responsibility and terror. I became adept at hiding my emotions. Survival demanded it.

Through it all, I learned about trust, or rather, the lack of it. My mum had betrayed me in ways I could barely understand at twelve. If I could not trust her, who could I trust? I relied on the small pockets of safety I could find and on my ability to navigate a world that seemed designed to hurt me. My grandmother became my anchor. Panda became a reminder of my lack of control. My mum was the constant force I had to endure.

The days blurred together in a cycle of obedience, fear, and brief respite. I cleaned, complied, endured, and survived. My voice mattered only when it aligned with the demands of the adults around me. Freedom was not given; it was taken away, piece by piece.

By the end of each day, I was exhausted emotionally and physically. I went to bed hoping the next day might bring some relief, some moment of safety, but most days it did not. Survival meant making choices I would rather not have to make. I learned early that freedom was something I could not take for granted.

I remember one particular evening when the house seemed especially oppressive. The living room smelled of stale alcohol, empty bottles littered the floor, and the noise of arguing adults filled every corner. I tried to tidy up quietly, stacking cans and wiping spilled drinks while Robert slumped on the floor in the kitchen, laughing or groaning; it was hard to tell which. My little sister was asleep upstairs, and I wanted to keep it that way. I wanted her to have a small fragment of normalcy that I could not enjoy. My mum came into the room, her eyes sharp and her voice cutting. She reminded me that I owed her compliance with Panda, that my refusal would bring only punishment. I nodded, even though my stomach churned with anger and fear.

I also began to notice patterns in my mum's behaviour. Her need to control me extended beyond Panda and her male friends. She watched my every move, punished small disobediences, and manipulated my feelings with both carrot and stick. If I did as she asked, even reluctantly, I was rewarded with small kindnesses or temporary peace. If I resisted, I was punished, grounded, or subjected to her cruelty. My life became a constant calculation, a balancing act of compliance and survival.

There were nights when I lay in the dark, staring at the ceiling, wondering why life had dealt me this hand. Fear, confusion, and sadness pressed down on me like a weight I could not lift. I tried to find answers, to understand why my mum, who was supposed to protect me, treated me this way. I could not comprehend her need to use me to satisfy her desires or to gain favour with her friends. I only knew that I had to endure, and I had to survive.

I also began to understand the nature of fear and compliance. Obedience was not about agreeing with what I was asked to do; it was about surviving, about protecting myself and my sister from harm. Each day was a lesson in calculating risk, in knowing when to speak, when to act, and when to stay silent. I learned to read the moods of adults, to anticipate their desires, to mask my true feelings behind a mask of compliance.

By the time this period ended, I had learned important lessons about survival, resilience, and autonomy. I had endured situations no child should face. I had learned to navigate fear, to read people, and to find small ways to protect myself and my sister. My mum's control and Panda's presence had stripped away my freedom, but they had also taught me the first lessons of resilience.

I learned that compliance could be a tool for survival, that small acts of defiance could preserve my sense of self, and that trust had to be earned. The months of forced relationships and lost freedom shaped my understanding of the world. They taught me to value moments of safety, to treasure acts of kindness, and to cling to the people who truly cared.

Looking back, I realise how much I learned about manipulation, control, and the human capacity for cruelty. But I also see the moments of hope, the small lights that guided me through the darkness. My grandmother's love, the small treats, the quiet evenings away from the chaos, they were my anchors. They reminded me that survival was possible and that one could endure even the worst circumstances.

By the end of this part of my life, I understood that my voice mattered, even if only in small ways. I learned to navigate fear, to protect my sister, and to survive in an environment designed to take my autonomy away. I learned that freedom was not given; it had to be found, even in tiny moments of choice and resistance.

I came through those months with a stronger sense of myself, even if it was buried under layers of fear and obedience. I learned to find joy in small things, to cling to moments of safety, and to recognise the people who truly cared. My grandmother's love, however brief, was proof that life could be different. Survival had given me lessons I would carry for the rest of my life: that obedience could be necessary, that small defiance could preserve dignity, and that even in the darkest times, hope could exist.

I emerged from this period not broken, but cautious, aware of the dangers in trusting too easily, and determined to carve out moments of control wherever I could. My childhood had been stolen in many ways, but I survived. And in that survival, I began to understand the first lessons of autonomy, resilience, and hope.

CHAPTER 6:
BETRAYED BY MY STEPFATHER

That night, I felt tense and terrified, waiting for something to happen, not knowing if I would be safe. I remember it was a Sunday night. My mum was in bed drunk again, and my little sister was asleep. Robert, my stepfather, and my cousin Kenny were in the lounge room watching *Mad Max*. About thirty minutes into the movie, Kenny said he was going home. I walked him to the door and let him out, trying to act normal, though a knot of fear had already formed in my stomach.

When I returned to the loungeroom and sat in the armchair, I noticed Robert staring at me. My heart started racing. I fiddled with my earring, trying to look busy, trying to be invisible. But he came over, knelt in front of me, and put his hands on my legs, rubbing them up and down. My stomach turned over. He whispered, "If you give me what I want, I'll give you anything."

I screamed, "Get away!" He moved back slightly, but panic surged through me, and I froze, unsure what to do next. My mum was drunk and asleep, completely unaware of what was happening. I couldn't risk running past him to get out the front door, and my own bedroom felt unsafe. My heart pounded as I considered my sister's room, thinking I might be safer there, though even that small hope was shadowed by fear and dread.

Her room had a single bed and a set of bunks. My sister slept in the single bed, so I climbed onto the top bunk, zipped myself into a sleeping bag up to my waist, and tried to hide. I didn't want to sleep, but eventually exhaustion overcame me. I woke in the night to find Robert rubbing my chest. I screamed again, "Get out!" He ran off. I stayed in the corner of the bunk bed, clutching the sleeping bag around me, until daylight. When I saw him leave through the back door, I ran to the neighbours' house, who were friends of Mum and Robert.

I told Irene what exactly had happened. She told me I had to tell my mum. I was scared to go back home; however, Irene offered to come with me. By the time we returned, Robert had already gone to work. I told my mum what had happened, and she asked if I was sure. I said yes. She replied, "Right, I'll take care of it." I felt a brief sense of relief. I thought that maybe I wouldn't have to be near him ever again.

At school, I tried to focus, but I was really exhausted. When I returned home that afternoon, everything changed. My mum grabbed me by the jumper and dragged me to the lounge room. Robert was sitting there. She said, "Now tell him what you told me." My words faltered as I repeated the story. Robert simply said, "I don't remember." He didn't deny it, but he didn't apologise either. My mum told me to get out of her sight. I ran to my bedroom. There was no tea, no comfort, only isolation.

The parties continued that week. On Friday night, I was woken multiple times to be paraded in front of mum's male friends. Robert lay on the lounge floor, drunk, and urinating himself again. My mum insisted I repeat the story exactly. I was scared, humiliated, and confused. She told me that if I had told anything differently, I'd have been "knocked down" and blamed for wearing a short school uniform. I went to bed that night feeling alone, terrified, and responsible for what had happened, thinking it was somehow my fault.

The following Monday, I fell asleep in class. The headmaster noticed and called me into his office. At first, he yelled at me for being tired, but as I broke down crying, he asked if things were okay at home. I couldn't answer at first. Eventually, I blurted out everything about Robert. He listened and promised to help me.

The next day, a woman came to my school and told me I couldn't go home because Robert was there. I was placed in a group home called *Roach Bank*, where two other girls were staying. Molly ran the home; it was strict, and she had her favourites, but I didn't mind. At first, it felt safe, even though I missed my sister terribly.

After five days, the guilt of leaving my sister behind became unbearable. She was still at home with Robert and Mum. I started worrying about her constantly: who would protect her? What if Robert hurt her the way he had hurt me? I felt I had no choice but to go back. I wanted to protect her, even if it meant risking myself.

Returning home was like stepping into hell again. Each night, I slept with three butter knives jammed into the door frame to keep Robert out. Even when mum asked if I had my knives, I thought she cared. But her words always followed with, "I don't want to hear any more of your lies." I felt completely alone. All I could focus on was keeping my sister safe.

Even though the group home had been safer, the guilt of leaving my sister at home drove me to act. I stayed vigilant, hyperaware of Robert's movements, and protective of my sister at every turn. My life had shrunk to survival and guarding her.

Returning home from the group home, I felt like I had stepped into a place where fear lived in every corner. I moved quietly, careful not to draw attention, but the constant worry for my sister gnawed at me. Nights were the hardest. I would lie awake, listening for any sound of Robert moving around, imagining the worst. I kept the knives jammed in the door frame, not trusting even a second that they would keep him out.

The parties never stopped. Every Friday and Saturday, the house is filled with men laughing, drinking, and leering. They looked at me in ways that made my stomach churn. I avoided eye contact, made myself small, and did everything I could to be invisible. Mum encouraged them while laughing, drinking, and showing no concern for what I had endured. I hated that she didn't see me as her daughter, just as a tool to maintain her life and her image in front of these men.

Robert was unpredictable. Some nights, he passed out drunk, sprawled across the lounge, leaving me to navigate the room carefully. Other nights, he would watch me, testing boundaries, reminding me that my safety was never guaranteed. I learned to move silently, to anticipate where he might be, and to find moments where I could breathe without being observed. My body tensed permanently, my nerves alert to every sound.

Mum's male friends added another layer of terror. They would stare, make comments, or expect me to comply with whatever mum instructed. I understood quickly that defiance could lead to punishment, but compliance didn't make me safe either. I was trapped between fear of Robert, fear of the men, and fear of my mum's response. Every day was a careful calculation, a balancing act where my sister's safety was my only focus.

Evenings were unbearable. I would check the locks, arrange the knives around the door frame, and lie in bed listening for any movement. I couldn't relax, couldn't sleep easily, and every sound made my heart race. My sister's safety was my responsibility, and I felt powerless. I couldn't control Robert or mum, but I had to try.

The emotional weight of being alone in this house was overwhelming. I couldn't tell anyone, couldn't trust anyone. Even the neighbours, as kind as they had been before, were no longer an option for ongoing protection. My mum's denial and her insistence that I tell Robert's friends exactly what had happened reinforced that I could trust no one. I began to feel that being a child was impossible here; every choice was about survival, every movement calculated to prevent harm.

During the days, I stayed in my bedroom, hiding under blankets, avoiding interactions, and watching my sister closely. I wanted her to have a childhood untouched by fear, but the reality was inescapable. Each day I watched her play, eat, and sleep, and I felt the tension between wanting to protect her and the fear that I might fail.

In those months, I also learned about the power of small acts. A locked door, a sleeping bag zipped around me, and even simply avoiding Robert's gaze became ways to survive. Every step, every movement had to be thought out, every word measured. I learned to trust my instincts because adults couldn't be relied on.

Despite it all, I never stopped thinking about my sister. I watched her sleep, checked she was okay, and made silent promises to protect her. I would endure anything to keep her safe. My focus was no longer on myself; it was entirely on her survival. The guilt of leaving her at the group home had reinforced this. I couldn't abandon her, even when fear was suffocating me.

Eventually, I realised the depth of mum and Robert's dysfunction. Their violent parties, their disregard for safety, and the way Robert treated me were all part of a pattern. Mum's focus was her social life, her friends, and her drinking. Her denial masked Robert's control and abuse. I learned to read their moods, anticipate the chaos, and manoeuvre through it as best I could.

I also realised that telling the truth didn't guarantee protection. When I had confided in the headmaster and social workers, I had been briefly taken to a group home, but returning home reminded me that no authority could enforce safety here. Survival was something I had to create myself, day by day, moment by moment.

Through it all, I developed a kind of resilience. I could no longer rely on anyone but myself and, in some ways, my little sister. I learned to navigate fear, anticipate danger, and protect what little I could. My life had become a series of calculations, and my innocence was gone, replaced by hyperawareness and responsibility that no child should bear.

Looking back, those months were not just about the abuse; they were about learning to survive in an environment designed to break me. I became adept at hiding, avoiding, and enduring. I discovered that even in the face of extreme fear, I could act, protect, and make choices that mattered. My sister's safety was the only measure of success I could rely on.

By the end of this period, I understood that fear could be endured, and that survival sometimes meant hiding, staying silent, and being strategic. I had learned lessons no child should have to learn, and yet I had to face them to protect the one person I loved more than myself. The house was full of danger, but I found ways to live within it, to survive, and to hold onto my sister's life as my own responsibility.

CHAPTER 7:
LIVING WITH STEVEN

Steven was one of my mother's male friends who would come to the house for the parties, but from the very beginning, he seemed different. Unlike the others, he never got rolling drunk, never shouted, and never created arguments. There was a calmness about him that felt almost impossible in our chaotic house. At first, I didn't know why I trusted him, why I felt a little relief when he was around, but over time, it became clear. He helped me with my homework a couple of times, showing patience when I struggled with things that should have been simple. It was the first time anyone had really tried to help me in that way without expecting something in return, and it left a small but lasting impression. Then he gave me his work telephone number. I remember feeling a strange mix of excitement and fear when I wrote it down, wondering if it was okay to call him, if it was safe, if anyone would find out. I started calling him every school day during my lunch hour, sometimes just to hear his voice, sometimes to ask questions about schoolwork, sometimes just to talk. His voice became a lifeline, a steadying presence in a life that was anything but stable.

In time, I started to feel a sense of safety around him, something I had not felt in years. There was a comfort in knowing someone was listening, someone who didn't yell or make me feel small. It was strange, this growing trust, because I had been taught to expect betrayal, disappointment, and fear from the adults in my life. And yet, with Steven, there was a patience and attentiveness I had never experienced. I could tell him things without fear of judgment, without being punished, without the usual anxiety that came with speaking at home. One night, when everyone else was drunk or had passed out, I finally let myself open up. I confided in him about what had been happening at home, about the fear, the confusion, and the ways I felt trapped and helpless. Even saying it out loud was terrifying; I had spent so long holding it inside that I wasn't sure it would be believed or even acknowledged, but he listened. He didn't shout or question me. He didn't turn away or dismiss me. He just listened.

That night, something shifted. The connection between us grew, slowly, carefully. I started to feel like maybe someone could care for me in a way I had never known. He became a kind of big brother at first, someone I could look to for guidance and support. There was a sense of being seen, of being acknowledged, that I had been starved of for years. I felt small relief, a flicker of trust, and a quiet hope that maybe, just maybe, not all adults were dangerous, that someone could be on my side. Over time, those feelings deepened, and I found myself relying on him more, leaning on his presence for a kind of emotional stability that I had never experienced before. It wasn't perfect; I was still cautious, still wary of being hurt, still scared of making mistakes. But with Steven, there was a glimmer of something I hadn't had in a long time: a sense that maybe I wasn't completely alone in the world.

I was 13 when we started having sex at my mum's house. I was in love with him and thought he loved me, even though I didn't really know what love was anyway.

My mum kicked me out one afternoon because I wouldn't do what she wanted. She wanted me to go to my friend's house and ask their mother for money so she could get alcohol. She was already drunk. I said no. She shoved me out the front door and said, "Get out, don't bother coming back."

I went to my friend Rayleen's house. She knew what was going on at home. She asked her mum if I could stay the night, and she said yes. The next day, I rang Steven. He met me, and I told him what had happened and that I had nowhere to go. He said he would take care of me.

He was living with his sister, her boyfriend, and her daughter. I moved in there with him; we shared a bedroom. I had to leave school to pay my way. I got a job at *Cheques Coffee Lounge*, making out I was 15. I was working in the kitchen. My pay cheque would go to Steven, and he would give me bus fares out of it to go and get back from work. I agreed with what he wanted; he was older than me, and I thought he knew what was best. I did what I had to so I could stay at his sister's place.

Friday and Saturday nights, Steven would go out, sometimes to my mother's, sometimes to other parties. I had to stay back. I didn't like staying behind, but had no choice. Strings were I had to have sex whenever he wanted it. I even had to role-play and make out I was someone else. I even had to make out that I was my mother. This made me sad, but I had nowhere else to go, so I went along with it. I hated it. There were a few nights Steven would bring other girls home. I would have to sleep on the lounge while they took my place in the bedroom.

I was 13 and a half when I became pregnant the first time. I was scared and happy, as I was told by a doctor that after my accident with the forklift truck, I might not be able to get pregnant. Steven was angry, and his sister said there was no room for a baby. If I were going ahead with the pregnancy, I'd have to find somewhere else to live.

The next day, once I got home from work, Steven sat me down and said I'd have to get an abortion. His sister had gotten her friend's identification, as I was underage, and said I had to go to Melbourne. I kind of agreed; I couldn't see any way out of it.

Two days later, I flew to Melbourne alone. I was so scared and sad that I couldn't even find my way out of Melbourne airport at the start. I got a taxi straight to Family Planning. I was an hour and a half early. I just sat in the waiting room. When the nurse, I presumed, came and got me, she gave me three tablets. I put a gown on, lay on a table, I felt sleepy, I dozed off for what seemed like a few minutes, and woke to the sound of a soft vacuum cleaner, but it wasn't. They had a device in me, making a sucking sound. I begged them to stop. The lady took my hand and said, "She's almost done." I was crying and was scared. I couldn't believe I had just gotten rid of my baby. This may have been the only chance I had to be a mother; I may not get another chance.

After that, they sat me in the waiting room. I paid the fee of $25. I rang Steven, told him it was done. He told me my mother had sent the police there, saying I had run away and that I was uncontrollable. Mind you, she kicked me out about 3 months ago. Steven told me it wasn't safe for me to return, so I ended up in Deloraine at my aunt's, but before long, the police came there. I had hidden outside in one of the barns for a few hours. I ended up giving myself up to the police.

They drove me to a group home called *Wybra Hall*. It was a boys' and girls' home. It shouldn't be called a home; it was hell. At first, it was okay. I could call Steven and talk to him. He even came and visited me. I had to go to court. My mother didn't show up, so I was sent back to *Wybra Hall*. This is when things started to change.

One night, in the middle of the night, two female workers woke me from my bed, took me to another room with just a bed in it, across from the laundry room. They locked me in. After a few minutes, I sat on the bed. A short time later, a male entered. He started putting his hands on me, pushing me on the bed. I fought back. He put his arms around my neck and forced me onto the bed, telling me to stop fighting him. I didn't. This seemed to go on for ages. He was strong. I gave a good fight, but in the end, he won and raped me.

The next day, I was left in there until about lunchtime. I was kept away from the others until the next day. I had bruising all around my neck. I was allowed back in with the other kids. This went on for a few weeks. There were a few nights I'd wake up in the middle of the night and notice one of the other girls was missing. I was relieved; it meant I was going to be left alone. Later on, I felt guilty for that.

I had to go back to court once again. My mother didn't show up. The judge released me from *Wybra Hall*. I was placed in another group home in the city. I left and went back to Steven.

CHAPTER 8:
BECOMING A MOTHER, CHOOSING LIFE

We also need to talk about my suicide attempt, which happened before my son was born. I was living back with Steven, his sister, her boyfriend, and her daughter. Nothing really changed: Steven still went to parties, I had to stay behind, and I still had to role-play. But I thought I was madly in love with him, even though he was 13 years older than me, so I did just about anything to keep him happy.

His sister, her boyfriend, and his daughter had gone away for the weekend. Steven said he wanted to break up with me, but he didn't give me a reason why. I begged him not to leave me. He said he wanted to have sex one more time; "goodbye sex," he called it. Once again, it was role-play where I had to pretend I was my mother. I remember crying during sex, begging him not to leave me. He told me to stop crying as I was ruining the role-play. Once he finished, he got off and told me to make him a cup of tea. I did. He was still telling me he was leaving me. I was living with him and his family, where was I supposed to go? I had no one.

I walked into the bathroom, opened the cupboard, took out the bottle of eucalyptus oil, and drank it, about half a bottle. Not long after that, Steven came into the bathroom and said he was ready to go one more time. I went into the bedroom, and the role-playing started again... I don't remember much after that, but I woke up in the hospital.

I spoke to Steven on the phone from the hospital. He told me that Kerry said I couldn't stay there anymore, and he was still leaving me. I spoke to the hospital staff, told them I had nowhere to go. They gave me numbers for a shelter; one was called Annie Kenny in Swan Street, North Hobart.

This version was for adults, but they agreed to take me in until they could find somewhere more suitable for my age. I left the hospital and went there. I called Steven and told him where I was, asking him to bring my clothing and things. When Steven arrived, I sat in the car and begged him not to leave me. He said he would give me one more chance, but I had to stay at Annie Kenny and could only go to stay with him on the weekends. I agreed.

Annie Kenny was horrible, but at least I had my own room. The other women would fight, some would come back drunk, and they always ran out of food. Later, they got me into Mara House, which was for kids my age. It was great; there were only five of us girls there. It felt safe and was clean. I started working at JB Automotive Products, which I loved. I would go to work each day, then back to Mara House. On weekends, I would stay with Steven.

After a while, I started feeling sick in the morning. I didn't think much of it at first, then I started to wonder: could I be pregnant again? I was excited and scared at the same time. I took about six pregnancy tests, and they were all positive. How do I tell Steven?

One of the workers at Mara House found one of my pregnancy tests and called me into the office. They told me they would have to make other arrangements for me, as they weren't equipped to have babies there. I felt very sad, as I loved being at Mara House and I felt safe.

That Friday night, Steven picked me up at seven as usual. I waited until we were in bed. I was role-playing for him again, and I blurted out that I was pregnant and this time I was keeping my baby. He got out of bed and said, "If you keep this baby, we are done." He took me back to Mara House. I was begging him not to leave us, but he did.

My mother came to Mara House and said she'd heard I was pregnant. She brought baby bibs and blankets and told me it was ok if I wanted to stay at my grandmother's. I hadn't reached out to my grandmother at first because I didn't want her in the middle, and coping with my mother's abuse. When my mother said I could go there, I was relieved. By this time, my mother and Robert had a daughter, Samantha.

I moved in with my grandparents and my uncle. My grandparents had their own room, and my uncle had one, so I had to sleep on the lounge, but I didn't mind. I loved being with my grandparents, so that to me was a small sacrifice. I would try calling Steven at work and at his home; he wouldn't speak to me. I gave his sister my grandparents' phone number, hoping he'd call.

Then one night he did. He asked me to meet him. I did. He said he wanted me back. I was so happy. My grandparents had been supporting me and helping me get things for my baby, as I was only receiving the Living Away from Home Allowance. Steven didn't help me get anything for our baby.

Things were back the way they had always been with Steven: sex, role-playing. I was six months pregnant when, after we finished having sex, he took me back to my grandmother's. The next morning, I woke up all wet. I said to my grandmother, "I think I wet myself." Then I told her I couldn't stop weeing. She asked me if my waters had broken. I said, "I don't know." She then asked, "Did fluid come out in a big rush?" I said, "No, it's just like a tap dripping."

That afternoon, I rang my specialist. He told me to come in, and he would check me out, so I did. He told me my water had broken, and I had to go to the hospital. I said, "Ok, I'll walk down." He said, "No, get a taxi." So I did. I was put on bed rest; I wasn't allowed to even get out of bed to go to the loo, as I was three months early. The nurse gave me injections to help my baby's lungs.

I was in the hospital for about three days. I started getting bad pains; I was in labour, and the hospital couldn't slow it down. I was rushed to the theatre. I was so scared and alone. I didn't know if my baby would even survive. I didn't want to lose another child.

When I woke, they told me I had a baby boy. He weighed 4 pounds 11 ounces. He was so tiny; he had to be tube-fed. I had a great milk supply. Steven came into the hospital and asked me to put our son up for adoption. I said no. "I had an abortion for you; I'm not getting rid of my son." He walked out of the hospital. I couldn't help but think, how could I do this on my own? I can barely take care of myself. But I knew I had so much love for my son, whom I ended up calling Steven.

I was 15 when I had my son. When my son was well enough to be released from the hospital, we both went back to my grandmother's and slept in the lounge room. It was hard at first. I didn't know anything about looking after a baby; I was always second-guessing myself, wondering if I was doing the right thing all the time.

My grandmother came to an appointment I had at Housing, the government housing department. They gave me a unit at Joseph Street, Rokeby. I got second-hand furniture. I was excited.

Steven would come down. We had an agreement that if I continued to sleep with him and do what he wanted in the bedroom, he would be a father to our son. I grew up without a father; I didn't want my son to, so I agreed.

I felt alone and isolated, as my grandmother lived in Montague Bay. I went back to Housing and put in for a transfer. I told them I wanted to be closer to her, as I did. It took about three months, then they offered me a place in Resolution Street, Warrane. It was three houses down on the other side of the road from Steven and his sister's place.

I moved in. Not long after, Steven would still come over some nights. I don't believe he was there to see his son; it was more for the sex, I believe. But I would try to get Steven to play with our son every chance I had.

I knew Steven was seeing other women. I didn't care, as long as he came and saw our son, even though I had to have sex and role-play for him to do that.

Then I fell pregnant again. I was on the pill. I was scared; I was 16. How was I going to take care of two kids under two years of age? Once again, Steven wasn't happy. He told me to give this child up for adoption, or he would leave, and our son wouldn't know who he was. I didn't want my son to grow up with no father, so in the end I agreed.

When my daughter was born, I didn't want to give her up. Steven came to the hospital and put more pressure on me, and some of the nurses also put pressure on me. I signed the adoption papers. Once home with my son, I couldn't stop thinking about my daughter, whom I named Charlene. I would cry myself to sleep at night.

Then, about a week later, the adoption centre sent me a photo of her. I contacted them, and apparently, there was a cooling-off period, so if I changed my mind, I could get her back. I rang them and told them I wanted my daughter back. She was so beautiful. I got her back. I didn't tell Steven.

Steven was due to come over. I fed my daughter, changed her, and settled her before he came over. I put her sleeping basket in the wardrobe with her in it and pushed the door not closed, but slightly open. I was scared.

When Steven arrived, he played with our son for about five minutes, then told me to put him to bed. I did. We entered my bed. We were getting into bed when Charlene woke up. Steven walked to the wardrobe, opened the door, and saw her. He looked at me and said, "I warned you what would happen," and he walked out the door.

I picked Charlene up and settled her down. I was upset, but at the same time was hoping Steven would change his mind, as he did with our son.

Days went by. I tried calling him and going over, but he didn't want to see us.

Then one night, just after I had settled both my children, there was a knock at the door. It was Steven. I was so happy to see him. I did the usual thing for him: sex, role-playing.

But this time, while we were in bed, Steven asked me if I could start sleeping with a few of his friends. He said they would pay me. I said no. This hit me hard, as I realised Steven never loved me. This time, I told him to get out. I was angry and hurt. How could I have ever thought that he loved me?

When my son was born, I remember he looked so sick; he was so tiny. I remembered thinking, "I can't lose him." When my daughter was born, I thought, "She's so beautiful." I always doubt myself as a mother. I loved my kids, but was I good enough to be their mother? That always played on my mind.

CHAPTER 9:
MEETING JOHN

After I left Steven, I moved out of my two-bedroom place in Resolution Street, Warrane, into a three-bedroom house in Hemskirk Street, Warrane. I started working at Ingenious, a jeans shop at Eastlands. During the week, I would drop Steven and Charlene at day care before work, then pick them up in the afternoon. We would go home, have baths, dinner, and follow the same routine each night. It felt good to have some structure in our lives.

One day, Darren came into the store. I knew him from the parties at my mum's house. He asked me out, and I agreed. After about two months of seeing each other, he invited me and the kids to spend a weekend at his sister's place in Oatlands. I thought it would be nice to get away.

Darren picked me up from work, and we collected the kids from day care before heading home to pack. The drive to Oatlands felt easy and normal. At first, the weekend seemed fine. After I settled the kids into bed, I had a couple of drinks of Stone Macs. Darren got annoyed when I said I did not want any more to drink, but I brushed it off.

When everyone else went to bed, Darren and I went to the sunroom where we were sleeping. Steven and Charlene were in a portacot in the same room. That was when Darren's mood changed. He started saying I was rude for not drinking more and accused me of thinking I was better than him. He began pushing me. I kept asking him to stop. Then he put his hands around my neck.

I remember looking over at my children, hoping they would not wake up. After that, everything went black.

When I came to my senses, I was on the floor, and my neck was sore. Darren was asleep on the bed. I realised I had wet myself. I felt ashamed, scared, and confused, but I knew I had to get out of there. I got changed quickly. My twin pram was in the lounge room. I picked up Steven first, then Charlene, as quietly as I could. I wrapped them in blankets, settled them into the pram, and left without waking Darren.

It was about three in the morning. It was dark and freezing. Every time a car went past, I hid in the bushes because I was terrified it might be Darren looking for us. Thank God it never was. The walk felt endless, but somehow we made it all the way back to Warrane.

Later that night, Darren came to my house. I did not open the door. I told him through the door that I did not want to see him again. He left and never came back. I took a few days off work because my feet were covered in blisters from the long walk.

During that time, I started thinking about how lonely I felt. I wished I had a normal relationship with my mum like my friends did with theirs. I wanted that connection so badly that I reached out to her and asked if she wanted to meet her grandchildren. She agreed. She was still with Robert. At first, I would only visit when I knew he was not home, and I never left my children there.

I slowly built a relationship with Samantha, the daughter Mum and Robert had together. She started staying with me most weekends and sometimes on weeknights, and I would take her back to school.

Then I found out that my sister Melissa, the one I had tried to protect when we were younger, was seeing Darren. I told her what he had done to me, but she did not want to hear it. She ended up having a child with him, and later he left her for her best friend, Leanne.

One Friday night, I went to pick Samantha up, and that was when I met John. He seemed nice, and we started chatting. The following week, Mum invited me inside when I came to get Samantha. Robert was there, and so was John. I kept my kids close to me, but John played with them and was good with them.

John and I began seeing each other away from my parents' place. At first, it was wonderful. I felt like I finally had the family I had always dreamed of. After about three months, I fell pregnant. I was excited. John did not have any children, and he was just as happy as I was when I told him.

For a while, everything felt right. Then, when I was about six months pregnant, things started to change. When John drank, he became abusive. He would pick on Steven and Charlene. I would put them in their bedroom and stand in front of the door so he could not get to them. Sometimes I would move a chest of drawers in front of the door and sit there with them, waiting for him to calm down. By morning, he would act as if nothing had happened.

I felt trapped, but I knew my most important job was to protect my children. I did the best I could.

After our daughter Danielle was born, his behaviour got worse. I would feed the kids, bathe them, and put them to bed before he came home, trying to keep them out of harm's way. Like clockwork, he would come home angry. One night, it was because there was a cup in the sink. He called me lazy and started hitting me. I would always put my hands over my face to protect it.

That night was worse than usual. He dragged me by the hair into our bedroom. He took off his shirt and growled at himself in the mirror, then looked at me and said, "What are those brats up to?" meaning my children. He walked towards their room. I ran after him and stood in front of their bedroom door. He knocked me down and dragged me back to our room by my hair.

He told me to get up and sit on the bed. I was crying, with my back to him. As I got up, he grabbed me by the back of the neck. He had a gun. I had never seen it before. He held it against my head. My eye was swollen, and my lip was bleeding.

He asked if I thought I was going to leave him. I was terrified and said no, telling him whatever I thought he wanted to hear, all while thinking about my children. He told me I made him hit me. I apologised and said I would try harder. Then he pressed the gun harder against my head. I begged him not to. I thought I was about to die. I closed my eyes, still crying.

Then there was a loud bang. I was too scared to open my eyes. I thought, oh my God, who did he shoot. I felt his hands tighten around my neck again, forcing me to look. My eyes reluctantly followed, and what I saw made my heart stop. A hole had been blown into the wall, a massive single hole surrounded by dozens of smaller cracks and fragments. The sound of splintering wood and falling debris still echoed in my ears, but worse was the sound of my children crying, their frightened voices piercing through the tension like tiny alarms. My stomach turned over. John's gaze was cold, calculating. He pointed at the shattered wall and said, "If you ever try to leave me, you get that," then gestured towards the direction of my children's bedroom. "Then they'll be next."

My entire body went rigid. Fear gripped me like a vice. I didn't hesitate. I ran as fast as I could to my children, who were trembling and crying. I scooped them into my arms, hugging them tightly, whispering soft reassurances even as my own chest heaved with panic. My hands shook uncontrollably, but I forced myself to be steady for them. I pressed kisses into their hair and murmured, "It's okay, I'm here. You're safe now." Inside, though, I felt anything but safe.

The next day, life tried to return to a semblance of normality. John appeared calm and unremarkable, acting as if nothing had happened. I knew better. I was terrified he would snap again at any moment. I couldn't trust anyone to help me. The black marks under my eyes were reminders of the previous night, and I feared that any intervention from others might provoke him. But I kept moving forward, holding the thin thread of routine together for my children.

A few weeks later, after receiving a payout from the accident with the forklift, a small sense of hope began to form. Maybe this was my chance to get away from him. I tried to live as normally as I could, maintaining a facade of calm, making sure Samantha, my sister, was safe whenever she stayed with us. John restrained his hands when she was around, likely knowing he could not show his true nature without witnesses. My mother noticed my black eyes on occasion, but never asked. I suppose it was easier for her to look away.

With determination, I bought an SLR 5000 car for ten thousand dollars, an important step toward independence. I also purchased a house in Rokeby. The removalists were booked, and John was at work. This was my moment. He knew where I was moving and the time the removalists would arrive, but John had no keys to the new place. It felt like the first real sense of safety I had experienced in months.

Once I arrived, Samantha and her friends stayed over that night to help unpack. I warned them that John would likely show up, but they insisted on staying to support me. As predicted, he did appear, demanding entry. I told him firmly that it was over. I would send any of his belongings to his parents and made it clear that I expected my car back. He was furious. The SLR 5000, which represented so much of my independence, became a weapon in our confrontation. John threatened that I would not get it back for weeks, revving the engine of my car in my driveway to intimidate me and my children. The noise and vibration made me flinch, my heart racing, but I refused to let him see my fear.

Days later, I discovered that Melissa, my sister, had moved out of our mother's house into a unit nearby. I had helped her furnish it, arranging for a lounge, kitchen table, and chairs, all while trying to protect my children from John. Then I learned the truth: she was seeing him. My stomach turned. I felt physically sick. She knew everything I had endured with him, and yet she had chosen to be with him. The betrayal cut deeper than anything I had felt from John himself. Not long after, she called my home, asking if John could see his daughter Danielle. I told her no, firmly, and hung up. I had to protect my children at all costs.

Meanwhile, I continued working with a lawyer to recover my SLR 5000 and resolve all matters with John. The repossession process moved forward, and I began to feel a glimmer of control returning to my life. On the day I received confirmation that everything with the car had gone according to plan, I was at my mother's house. Through the kitchen window, I saw John walking past with a six-pack in hand, yelling abuse at me. My body instinctively recoiled, and I moved away from the window.

About an hour and a half later, I received the call confirming that the car had been successfully repossessed. Relief washed over me, but it was only temporary. I was leaving my mother's house with her in the front seat, my three children in the back, and Samantha beside them. We were driving to my own home when I noticed a car tailing us. John was behind us, following closely, attempting to intimidate me. He kept pulling up beside my car, then falling back, then coming up again. Each time, I gripped the steering wheel tighter, my knuckles went white.

We made it to the house, barely, and I ran inside with the kids. I tried to call the police repeatedly, as did my mother, but the lines were busy. Then the nightmare escalated. John began smashing the front windows of the house. My children screamed in terror. I tried to comfort them, holding them tightly, whispering that everything would be okay, even as my own chest shook with panic. I could not believe this was happening again. The sense of safety I had fought so hard to create was crumbling before my eyes.

I was desperately trying to comfort my children, holding them close as John's rage continued to escalate. He had already smashed every window in the loungeroom, shards of glass scattered across the floor, glittering dangerously in the light. The sound of splintering wood and shattering glass echoed through the house. My heart was hammering in my chest, my mind racing for any way to protect my children. He turned his attention to the front bedroom windows next, hurling himself against them until the glass cracked and fell in jagged pieces.

Then he came to the front door. My mother was frantically trying to call the police, but the lines were all busy, and the tension was unbearable. I could hear the kids crying behind me, their tiny voices rising in panic. Suddenly, the side window next to the door exploded, sending glass raining down around us. Not long after, the three glass panels in the front door shattered under his attack. My children screamed, and I instinctively scooped them up, shielding them as best I could, pressing them against my body to protect them from the chaos.

John forced his way in, one hand prying the door open, the other gripping a knife. My heart skipped a beat. My mind screamed at me to protect my children. Adrenaline surged through me. I grabbed the gun I had, pointing it directly at him. My body was trembling, but I couldn't let fear paralyse me. As Steven ran past me, John lunged and grabbed him. "Let him go!" I shouted, my voice cracking with panic. John sneered, "Or what?" My son's terrified cries echoed in my ears. I pointed the gun at him, and it went off. The recoil sent me staggering back, my shoulder burning from the impact, and in the chaos, the gun struck John in the groin.

He released Steven but stepped forward aggressively. I reacted instinctively, bashing the gun over my leg, just as I had seen in the movies. Miraculously, it opened, allowing me to reload. Steven clung to my leg, frightened but unharmed. John, frustrated and injured, retreated outside and collapsed on the lawn. My sister Melissa was with him, silently watching. I placed the gun on the bench and sank to the lounge room floor, holding my children tightly, trying to calm their shaking bodies.

When the police arrived, they immediately assessed the situation. "Who shot John?" they asked. I said simply, "I did." They handcuffed me, but it felt surreal. I was relieved that my children were safe. We waited anxiously for the ambulance to take him away. In front of that, once at the police station, one officer, Sergeant Carrick, kindly offered me a can of Coke and a Mars bar to help me calm down. I felt the weight of the world pressing on me, convinced I was going to jail and that I would lose my children forever.

After giving my statement, the police confirmed I would not be charged for defending myself and my children. I was only charged with letting a firearm off in a suburban area. John's injuries were severe; he had lost part of his left leg from the knee down and his left testicle. Later, I was called to give evidence in court. I had to demonstrate how I had pointed the gun at him, how I had opened it to reload. I explained to the court that I had bashed it over my leg as I had seen in the movies, and although there was apparently a lever I should have pressed, my desperate action had worked. They showed pictures of my leg, bruised and purple from bashing the gun open. That day marked the last time I saw John.

The betrayal that cut deepest came from my sister, Melissa. She had known that I had my children there and that John had a history of violence, yet she arrived with him. I had spent my life trying to protect her, guiding her, and keeping her safe. For her to bring John into my home, knowing he could and would threaten my children, was unforgivable. I have not spoken to her since, and I doubt I ever will. From what I understand, she has had three sons with John, though they are no longer together. My relationship with her is irreparably broken.

Even now, years later, the aftermath of those events weighs heavily on me. I feel sorrow for Danielle, my daughter, who grew up with three half-brothers who are also her cousins. She should never have had to navigate a family torn apart by violence and betrayal. These events should never have happened. I did everything I could to protect my children, and I can only hope that by telling this story, I can make sense of it all and ensure that the next generation knows safety and love in ways I fought so hard to provide.

CHAPTER 10:
BEING WITH PHILLIP

I started going out on Friday and Saturday nights with my friends. We would go to nightclubs to dance, laugh, and have a few drinks. It felt like freedom, those nights. Like I could be someone other than just a mum drowning in responsibility. Samantha, my sister, was still in high school, so she would babysit my three children, and sometimes one of her friends would stay over too. I always made sure my children were fed, bathed, and, most of the time, asleep before I left. That mattered to me. Even when I was struggling, even when everything else felt like it was falling apart, I needed to know they were cared for before I walked out that door. It was the only way I could let myself leave without the guilt eating me alive.

One night, my friend Joanne Francome and I went to the Empire Hotel. The music was great, the atmosphere was electric, and we danced until we were breathless. I was feeling light, carefree, like for a moment I could forget everything else in my life. The weight I carried every other minute of every day seemed to lift, just for those few hours. As I went to get a drink, I noticed a man at the bar watching me. He spoke to me; his name was Phillip. He asked if I was having a good night. I smiled and said yes. There was something in his eyes that felt like attention, like interest, and God, I hadn't felt that in so long. Then he asked if I was alone. I said no, I was with my friend Joanne. He laughed, and I asked why. He said he meant if I was with a guy. I told him no, I was single, and then returned to the dance floor, trying not to overthink it. But my heart was beating faster, and I felt something I hadn't felt in a while. Hope, maybe, or the possibility of it.

As the night began to wind down and people started leaving, Joanne and I sat at the bar. Phillip came over, chatting casually with us. He was charming. Easy to talk to. Before we left, he asked if I wanted to meet up the next night. I agreed without hesitation. That simple moment felt like a spark, like maybe something good could happen for me. Like maybe I wasn't just a single mum struggling to keep her head above water. Maybe I could be wanted. The following week, we caught up again, and the week after that, Phillip came home with me.

At first, he was fun. He made me laugh and brought some lightness into my life. He was good to my children, and I felt like I could finally breathe a little. We would watch movies together, listen to music, and just enjoy small moments of happiness. For a while, I let myself believe this could work. That maybe I'd found someone who wouldn't hurt me, who could be a partner. But Phillip had a pager that constantly went off, and he would disappear, sometimes ten times a day, only for short periods. When I asked where he had to go, he would brush it off, saying he had things to take care of. His tone would shift, just slightly, enough to let me know not to push. Later, I learned he was selling drugs, and whenever the pager rang, he would meet his customers. The knowledge sat heavily in my chest, but I convinced myself it didn't matter. I told myself people did what they had to do to survive.

For the first eighteen months, things seemed manageable. I could almost pretend we were normal. But the violence slowly crept in, like water seeping under a door. If I didn't agree with him or upset him in some small way, he would fly off the handle. The shift would happen so fast I barely had time to brace for it. One moment we'd be talking, and the next his face would darken, his voice would rise, and I'd know what was coming. My children would rush to their rooms once the shouting and crashing started.

I hated that they knew the warning signs. I hated that they had learnt to recognise the sound of danger. I tried desperately not to make any noise, to shield them from what was happening, but the fear was constant. It lived in my throat, in my chest, in the way I held my breath whenever Phillip walked into a room.

There were nights I would fall to the ground under the force of his blows, covering my face as best I could, praying it would stop. His kicks and punches were relentless. Each one felt like it was trying to break something inside me that was already barely holding together. I remember the dull thud of his fist connecting with my ribs, the sharp crack when his boot caught my leg. I remember the metallic taste of blood in my mouth, the way my ears would ring after he hit my head. But worse than the physical pain was the feeling of being trapped, of knowing there was nowhere to go, no one coming to save me. I felt like an animal backed into a corner, just waiting for the blows to stop so I could crawl away and survive another day.

One night, Phillip beat me so severely that when the ambulance arrived, I couldn't even get off the ground. I remember lying there, numb, terrified, and humiliated, wondering how my life had come to this, how my children were witnessing pieces of this pain even when I thought I had shielded them. The paramedics' voices felt distant, like they were speaking to me through water. I couldn't focus on their questions. All I could think about was whether my children had heard me screaming, whether they were frightened, and whether they thought I was going to die. Every thump, every strike, every moment of violence left marks not just on my body but deep in my mind. I became hyper-aware of every sound, every movement, every shift in his mood. A door closing too hard. A plate set down with too much force. The scrape of a chair. All of it became a potential warning. I learnt to anticipate the violence, to hide, to survive, not just for myself but for my children, who depended on me to protect them from the world I couldn't control. But I couldn't even protect them from what was happening inside our own home.

Another time, he punched me in the head with so much force that he actually broke his own hand. I remember the shock of that, not concern for him, but disbelief at the level of violence it took to do that much damage. His hand swelled badly, turning purple and grotesque, and he ended up needing surgery. I stared at his hand and thought about how hard he must have hit me for the bone to break. Even then, even injured, he still blamed me. It was always my fault somehow. I was too mouthy. I didn't listen. I provoked him. The accusations became a script I knew by heart, one that played over and over until I started to believe it myself.

There was another night when he hit me so hard I lost consciousness. I don't remember falling, only the blackness swallowing me whole, a kind of silence that felt almost peaceful compared to the chaos. When I came to my senses, I felt something wet on my face. For a moment, I was confused, disoriented, trying to understand where I was. My head pounded. My vision was blurred. Then I realised, Phillip was urinating on me while I lay there helpless. The humiliation of that moment cut deeper than the bruises. It wasn't just violence anymore. It was degradation. It was him showing me that I wasn't even human to him. I felt erased. Like I was nothing, I remember lying there, too weak to move, too broken to cry, just feeling the warmth of his urine on my skin and wishing I could disappear entirely. That moment stayed with me for years. It still does.

The beatings were horrific, but what made it harder to escape was that they didn't happen all the time. There were stretches where things felt almost normal. He could be charming, funny, even gentle. He'd bring me flowers, apologise, tell me he loved me, promise it would never happen again. Those periods of calm kept me hoping, kept me thinking, If I just don't upset him... If I say the right thing... if I stay quiet... then maybe the violence wouldn't come back. I started measuring my life by his moods, walking on eggshells in my own home, trying to predict storms before the clouds even formed. I became obsessed with reading him, watching for the smallest signs. But no matter how careful I was, the violence always came back. It was never a question of *if*, only *when*.

Phillip began using drugs in front of me, offering them like they were nothing, like they were a normal part of life. He'd sit on the lounge with a spoon and a lighter, cooking up whatever he had that day, and he'd ask if I wanted some. I always said no. I was already prescribed morphine for legitimate medical reasons, and I took it exactly as my doctor instructed. I was strict about that. It was one of the few things I still felt I had control over. I told myself I would never cross that line. Using drugs the way Phillip did felt like giving up completely, and I wasn't ready to do that yet.

One day, though, I asked him what was so different about using it his way. He said it made you forget, forget the pain, forget the fear, forget everything bad. He said it like it was the most natural thing in the world, like forgetting was a gift. At the time, I didn't understand how tempting those words would become. But they planted a seed in my mind, one that would grow every time he hurt me, every time I felt like I couldn't take another day.

For years, I kept refusing. I held onto that boundary like it was the last piece of myself I hadn't lost. Then one night, he beat me so badly I couldn't get out of bed the next day. Every part of me hurt: my ribs, my face, my legs. I could feel bruises forming on bruises, layers of pain that seemed to go deeper than skin. But the worst pain was inside, the hopelessness that sat heavy in my chest. I felt trapped in a life that was just survival from one day to the next. I remember lying there, staring at the ceiling, thinking about how I used to have dreams. I used to want things. Now I just wanted the pain to stop.

That was the moment I gave in.

The first time I misused the morphine, I remember the warmth spreading through my body, starting in my toes and rising slowly upward until it wrapped around my head like a blanket. The noise in my mind went quiet. The fear dulled. The memories blurred. For the first time in a long while, I didn't feel terror sitting just under my skin. I felt... nothing. And nothing felt like relief. It felt like the first breath of air after being underwater for too long.

Phillip had been right about one thing; it made me forget. But what I didn't realise then was that it would also take everything else from me. My clarity. My emotions. My ability to fight back. My sense of who I was.

Before long, I was dependent. What started as an escape became a need, a hunger that sat in my bones. The abuse didn't stop, but it felt distant, like it was happening to someone else. I would watch Phillip's fist coming towards my face and feel almost detached, like I was watching a movie. I stopped fighting back emotionally. I stopped reacting. I would endure it and then move through the rest of the day in a fog. Numbness replaced fear, and in a strange way, that felt like relief. But it wasn't relief. It was a surrender. It was me giving up piece by piece.

I remember one night we went out, and Phillip disappeared from the pub, leaving me there alone. I didn't even look for him. I just went home. I didn't have the energy to care anymore. I sat on the lounge in the dark, not even bothering to turn on the lights, and I thought about how empty I felt. That scared me, the way my feelings were shutting down. I used to cry when he hurt me. Now I barely blinked.

When he came home later, he broke in through the laundry window. I was asleep when he started hitting me. I woke up to pain exploding across my face, not even fully aware of what was happening at first. My brain couldn't catch up to the assault. There was blood everywhere, on the sheets, on the pillow, on my clothes, dripping onto the floor. I tasted it, thick and metallic in my mouth. When I finally looked in the mirror the next morning, I barely recognised myself. My face was swollen and bruised, one eye nearly closed, my lip split open. No amount of make-up could hide it. I looked like I had been in a boxing ring and lost. Badly.

Inside, though, I felt even worse. I felt empty. Hollow. The drugs had taken my fear, but they had also taken my strength, my voice, and my sense that I deserved better than this. I looked at my reflection and didn't even feel sad anymore. I just felt... gone.

I coped with the abuse by using more drugs because they stopped me from feeling. They did not just dull the pain in my body; they numbed everything inside me. Fear, sadness, shame, even love started to feel far away, like emotions happening to someone else. There was a time when I truly believed I deserved the way he treated me. I thought if I could just be better, quieter, more patient, then maybe someone would love me properly. Maybe I wouldn't be such a burden. My self-worth was so low that I blamed myself for the violence if I hadn't said that. Suppose I hadn't looked at him wrong if I'd just kept my mouth shut. The drugs made those thoughts easier to live with. They wrapped my mind in a fog where nothing felt quite real. I could float through my days without really being present, and that felt safer than facing the truth of what my life had become.

Then I found out I was pregnant, not with one baby but with twins. The moment I knew, something inside me shifted. Through all the numbness, I felt fear for them. Real, sharp, undeniable fear. I knew I could not keep using drugs and carry two babies safely.

The thought of them being born dependent, of them suffering because of my choices, broke through the fog in a way nothing else had. For the first time in a long while, I wanted to fight for something. Not for me, but for them. I joined a methadone programme and went to the chemist every single day. I had to drink my dose in front of them, standing at the counter, while they watched to make sure I swallowed it. It was humiliating, standing there with people staring, knowing they were judging me, knowing what they must think of me. But I did it because my babies mattered more than my pride. They mattered more than anything.

When I was about seven months pregnant, Phillip's violence became even more terrifying. One night, he knocked me to the floor. I fell hard, my belly hitting the ground, and panic shot through me. I tried to roll onto my side to protect them, but Phillip was standing over me. He was holding a kitchen knife, the blade catching the light, and screaming that he would cut his babies out of me. I have never felt fear like that in my life. It was beyond terror. It was primal, a kind of fear that made my whole body shake. I truly believed I was going to die and that my unborn children would die with me. I could feel them moving inside me, oblivious to the danger, and I thought about how they would never take a breath, never feel sunlight, never know anything but this. I was crying, begging him to stop, trying to curl my body around my belly to protect them, my hands spread across my stomach as I could somehow shield them from a knife.

Samantha was home that night. My other children were asleep in their beds, and I prayed they stayed asleep, that they wouldn't hear this, that they wouldn't come out and see. When Samantha saw what was happening, she threw herself over me, covering my stomach with her own body and screaming at Phillip to leave me alone. Her body was warm against mine, and I felt her shaking, felt her fear mixing with mine. I was terrified he would hurt her, too. She was just a kid herself, and she was putting herself between a man with a knife and me. I tried to push her away because I did not want her to be injured, because I couldn't bear the thought of him hurting her because of me, but she refused to move. She clung to me, crying, shouting at him to stop.

When I lifted my arm to shield us, Phillip slashed downward with the knife and cut my arm. I remember the sharp sting, like a line of fire across my skin, and then the warm feeling of blood running down, soaking into my sleeve. The pain was immediate and bright, but it was nothing compared to the fear of what could have happened.

I grabbed a tea towel and wrapped it tightly around my arm, my hands shaking so badly I could barely tie it. Blood seeped through the fabric almost immediately. Samantha ran to the kitchen window and pushed it open, the cold night air rushing in. She told me to climb out before he killed me. She was crying, her voice high and desperate, and I could see the terror in her eyes. I was crying too, asking about the children. I couldn't leave without them. Samantha promised she would get them. She looked me in the eyes and promised, and I trusted her. I had to.

I climbed out the window, shaking, bleeding, my belly making it hard to move, and I ran for help. My bare feet slapped against the pavement, the cold biting at my skin, but I didn't stop. I could hear my own breathing, ragged and panicked, and I thought about my babies with every step. Phillip ran out the front door and disappeared into the night. At the hospital, they stitched my arm, the needle pulling through my skin over and over, and checked the babies. I lay there shaking, not from pain but from the shock of how close we had come to dying. The doctor asked me what happened, and I couldn't find the words. I just shook my head and cried.

After the twins were born, Phillip and I were both still on methadone programmes, but he continued to use drugs on the side. For a while, I slipped back into old habits too. The exhaustion of two newborns, the constant crying, the sleepless nights, the feeling of being overwhelmed, it all pulled me back under. I hated myself for it, but addiction had its grip on me, especially when I felt overwhelmed or afraid. Every time I told myself I wouldn't use, I'd find myself doing it anyway, as my body moved on its own. The shame of that was crushing.

One day, Phillip was in the lounge room while our daughter Stephanie was on the floor playing. He was scraping the coating off morphine pills, his focus entirely on the task, the little shavings falling onto the table. I left briefly to check on James, who was crying in the other room, then came back. Phillip went to the toilet and returned, asking where the other pill had gone. I said I did not know. He pointed near his briefcase on the floor, right where Stephanie had been playing. Stephanie had been playing right there.

My heart dropped. The world seemed to stop. I rushed to her and saw she had the pill in her mouth, her little fingers sticky, her face curious. Time seemed to stop. Everything else disappeared: the noise, the room, Phillip, everything except my daughter and that pill. I pulled it out, my fingers shaking, and washed her mouth, running my finger over her gums, checking her tongue, shaking so badly I could barely hold her. I remember yelling at Phillip, my voice raw and desperate, asking how he could be so careless, how he could put his own child in danger. The rage I felt in that moment was hotter than any fear I'd ever experienced. But underneath the anger was something stronger. It was clarity.

In that moment, I knew I had to leave him. Not tomorrow, not one day, but as soon as I could. My children were not safe, and if I stayed, I was choosing a life that could destroy them. I was choosing drugs and violence over their futures. That realisation cut through the fog in my head stronger than any drug ever had. It was like a light switching on in a dark room, sudden and blinding.

I tried to leave Phillip many times, but leaving him was never simple. If I asked him to go, he would refuse, his voice calm and cold, like he was explaining something obvious to a child. If I left the house with the children, packing bags in a rush while they cried and asked where we were going, he would break in while we were gone and be there when we got back, sitting on the lounge like he owned the place, as if nothing had happened. I felt like there was no safe space where he could not reach me. No matter how many locks I changed, how many times I told him to leave, he always found a way back in. Even when I gathered the courage to walk away, he always found a way back in. It felt like being trapped in a maze with no exit.

My sister Samantha once told me she came over and found him injecting me with drugs while I was already out of it on the couch. She said I was unconscious, my body slack, and he was tying off my arm like it was nothing. Hearing that later made me feel sick to my stomach, bile rising in my throat. I had been so deep in addiction and emotional pain that I was not even aware of what was happening to my own body. I had no control. I was a puppet, and he was pulling the strings. That realisation still haunts me. I was not just being hurt by him; I was disappearing inside myself, piece by piece, until there was almost nothing left.

When Phillip would turn violent, I called the police; one car was never enough. There would be two or three carloads of officers just to handle him, their radios crackling, their voices urgent. The neighbours would watch from their windows and doorways, the lights flashing outside, painting everything red and blue, and I would feel shame on top of fear. Shame that everyone knew. Shame that they could see what my life had become. But even that did not keep him away for long. As soon as things calmed down, he would come back around, knocking on the door or calling through the window, asking for my medication, trying to pull me back into the same cycle. And sometimes, God help me, I let him.

Sometimes I lied and told him I had sold my tablets just so he would leave. I would make up stories about who I'd sold them to, how much I'd got, anything to make him go away. I felt trapped in a life I did not recognise anymore. The woman I used to be, the one who had dreams, who laughed easily, who believed in love, felt like a stranger. I couldn't even remember what she looked like.

The only way I finally managed to break free was by starting another relationship, because Phillip had said the only way he would let me go was if I belonged to someone else. Those were his exact words. "You're mine until someone else takes you." Even that decision came from fear, not love. I just wanted him out of my life. I wanted to stop looking over my shoulder. I wanted to stop flinching every time I heard footsteps.

Looking back now, I know using drugs to forget was one of the worst choices I made, even though at the time it felt like the only way to survive. The drugs helped me block out the pain, the fear, and the constant anxiety, but they also took away my emotions. I became numb to everything, even the things that should have mattered most. Joy. Love. Connection. Hope. All of it disappeared into the fog.

My children were fed, they were clean, and they had a roof over their heads, but they did not have all of me. I was there in body, but not always in heart or mind. I went through the motions, making meals, doing laundry, putting them to bed, but I wasn't really present. I regret that more than anything. More than the drugs, more than staying with Phillip, more than any of the choices I made. I do not think I told them I loved them enough during that time. I do not think I showed them the warmth and safety they deserved. I don't remember cuddling them as much as I should have. I don't remember playing with them, really playing, getting down on the floor and losing myself in their world. They were innocent, and none of what was happening was their fault. They didn't ask to be born into that chaos. They deserved a mother who was whole, who was present, who could protect them. Instead, they got a version of me that was barely surviving.

For a long time, I believed I had failed as a mother. The word "failure" sat in my chest like a stone, heavy and immovable. I still carry guilt for those years. It's a weight I don't think I'll ever fully put down. They deserved better than the version of me that addiction and abuse had turned me into. They deserved laughter and safety and stability. They deserved a home that felt like a sanctuary, not a war zone. No matter how much I have changed since then, I cannot get that time back. That is one of the hardest truths I have had to learn to live with. Time doesn't rewind. Childhoods don't get do-overs. And those years are gone forever.

My twins James and Stephanie

CHAPTER 11:
LOSS OF A CHILD

I did not jump into Leigh's arms because I loved him. I want to be honest about that, even if it is one of the hardest truths I have had to carry. I moved toward him because I was running away from someone else. Phillip had consumed years of my life with his violence, his jealousy, and his relentless ability to find me wherever I tried to hide. I was exhausted in a way that went beyond tired. It was the kind of worn-down that settles into your bones and makes you wonder whether you will ever feel safe again. When I thought about Leigh, I thought about escape. I thought about a door that Phillip could not kick in. I thought about sleeping without one ear open.

Leigh and I had a history of a kind. I had known him from my days living on Resolution Street in Warrane, years before any of this. He was familiar, and familiarity can feel like safety when everything else is chaos. He was willing to take on my five children and me, and I want to acknowledge what that meant. He knew the situation I was coming from. He knew I was still on the methadone programme. He stepped in anyway, and I am grateful for that part of him, even though what came later would strip much of that gratitude away.

But Phillip did not disappear just because I had moved on. That is not how men like Phillip operate. They do not respect new chapters. They do not respect boundaries, restraining orders, or locked doors, or the fact that you have built something new and want to live in it peacefully. He would come around smashing windows. He would find us at caravan parks and show up screaming, and the police would come and remove him, and I would feel that brief flicker of relief before the caravan park manager would turn to me and say that I had to leave. Not Phillip, but my children and I were the inconvenience.

I remember the particular indignity of that, the way it made me feel like we were the ones causing trouble simply by existing and being targeted. We moved from hotel to hotel, caravan park to caravan park, trying to stay one step ahead of a man who had appointed himself the architect of my misery. My children were frightened. I could see it in the way they moved, always cautious, always half-braced for the next explosion. Children should not have to live that way. I knew it, and I felt the weight of it pressing down on me every single day.

By the time welfare stepped in, I was four months pregnant to Leigh. I had been on the injection as contraception, but it had not worked. Welfare looked at my situation with clear eyes and saw what I had been too close to see clearly myself. I did not have a stable home for my children. We were here one week and somewhere else the next. There was no consistency, no routine, no sense of a foundation beneath their feet. They were right. I hated that they were right, but they were.

My children went into care. I agreed to it. I want people to understand that I agreed to it, because sometimes I think people picture a woman who had her children taken against her will, and that is not entirely the picture. I chose to let them go because I believed, in that moment, that it was the safest option for them. But agreeing to something and being okay with it are two very different things. The moment they left, something inside me fractured. Not broke. Fractured. In the way that a bone can fracture in multiple places and still hold a shape, even though every movement afterwards hurts.

I failed them. That was the thought that circled my mind day and night without mercy. Not the thought that I had tried, or that I had been in an impossible situation, or that I had made the only choice available to me. Just that one sentence, repeating: *I failed them*. I could not sleep without it. I could not wake up without it. I could not eat a meal or walk down a street without that sentence following behind me like a shadow I could not outrun. There was guilt layered over grief, layered over shame, layered over a kind of love so fierce it felt like it was tearing me open from the inside.

And underneath all of that was a feeling I did not know how to name for a long time, one I felt deeply ashamed of. I knew my children were physically safer without me, in that moment. They were being cared for. They had a stable roof over their heads. And yet that knowledge brought me no peace whatsoever. I could not be grateful for their safety because they were not with me, and I kept telling myself that I should feel grateful, that I should feel relief, but the fact that I felt neither made me feel like an even worse mother. The grief at losing them was not something I could logic away. It lived in my body as much as my mind.

When the police came to where I was staying, I was eight months pregnant. They had a warrant. I was twenty-five dollars short of the amount listed on it. *Twenty-five dollars*. I want you to hold that number for a moment, because I have held it for years. Twenty-five dollars was the difference between a pregnant woman staying home that night and a pregnant woman being handcuffed and loaded into the back of a paddy wagon.

They cuffed my hands behind my back. I had to shuffle across the floor of that vehicle and lower myself down with no hands to catch myself, my belly enormous and awkward, every movement slow and humiliating. The officers were not kind. I remember that clearly. They were not cruel in a dramatic way. They were simply indifferent, which in its own way is a kind of cruelty. I was a number to be processed, not a heavily pregnant woman who was frightened and in an impossible situation.

They took me to the hospital prison. They removed my shoelaces, which is such a strange detail to remember, but I do. I was put in a room with a bed and a toilet. The room was dirty. At some point that night, I started getting pains in my stomach. I called out. An officer came in. When I told her about the pains, she asked if I was in labour. I told her I did not know because I had always had caesarean sections and had never experienced labour. She told me that if I were in labour, I would know. She said it in that dismissive tone people use when they have already decided not to take you seriously.

At one point, I needed to use the toilet, but there was no toilet paper. I told the officer. She told me toilet paper cost a dollar and ten cents, which I did not have. I have never forgotten that detail either. Eight months pregnant, in pain, in a dirty cell with no shoelaces, and I could not even have toilet paper because I didn't have one dollar and ten cents to pay for it. These are the small humiliations that compound into something much larger. They remind you of exactly how much you matter to a system that is supposed to protect you.

The next morning, I stood before the judge. I told him I had been twenty-five dollars short of the fine. He was horrified. He released me that morning, and I could see in his face that he understood how wrong it all was. But understanding something is wrong does not undo it. I went home, showered, and lay down. Later that day, I went to the hospital. I had an infection. My baby had no heartbeat.

They told me I would have to give birth naturally. I did not understand. Every birth I had ever had was a caesarean section. I had no frame of reference for what they were telling me. And I think on some level, I did not believe them about the heartbeat. I thought they must have made a mistake. I held onto that thought with everything I had, because the alternative was something I could not yet allow myself to look at directly.

I gave birth to my daughter later that day. I named her Wendy. When she came out, I thought for one precious moment that I heard her cry. She was very dark and very tall. She was placed in my arms, and I held her. Then I looked at her face, and she was beautiful. Later, I had to be rushed to the theatre because the placenta had become stuck and needed to be surgically removed. Before they took me, I told Leigh not to let anyone take my baby. I meant it. I was not ready. I did not care what they said. I was not ready.

When they put me in a room after the operation, Wendy was with me. I could hear all the other babies crying in that ward. All the other babies, with their noise and their need, the ordinary beautiful chaos of new life. Mine was silent. I held her for days. I kept waiting for her to stir. I kept watching her face in the way new mothers watch their babies, looking for small movements, small signs. Welfare wanted to bring my other children in to meet their sister. I said no. I was not ready for that either. I needed the time inside that room to belong just to us.

When the nurses told me it was time for Wendy to go to the morgue, I would not let them take her. I understand now what they were seeing that I was refusing to see. A mother in denial, clutching her baby, unable to let go. But in that moment, all I knew was that she was my daughter and no one was going to take her from me. It was only after a few more days, when I could no longer ignore what was happening, when I could smell what grief really smells like, that I finally understood. She was really gone. She had always been gone. I had just not been able to live inside that truth yet.

I blamed myself. The blame came immediately and settled in deeply, the way water settles into the cracks of a rock. I had had an abortion at some point before this. My children were in welfare care. I was still on the methadone programme, even though my doctor had told me clearly that the methadone had not caused Wendy's death. I heard the words. I did not believe them. I had constructed a narrative in which God was punishing me, and once you have built that narrative, it is very hard to pull down. I was not being irrational, not entirely. I was a woman who had done things she regretted, who had made choices she wished she could take back, and who had now lost a child. The human mind looks for reasons. It looks for cause and effect, for some order inside the chaos. The reason I arrived at was myself.

I went to grief counselling. They told me it would get easier. I want to say something clearly about that: it does not get easier. That is not the truth. What happens, if you are lucky, if you survive long enough, is that you learn to carry it differently. The weight does not lessen. You just build more muscle for holding it. The counsellors meant well, but every time they told me it would get easier, I felt more alone, because I could feel that it would not, and I thought perhaps something was wrong with me for feeling that way.

I stopped seeing my other children on weekends. I know how that sounds. I know it sounds like abandonment, like failure compounded on failure. But the truth was more complicated than that, as the truth usually is. I was terrified of letting them down again. I had already let them down so many times, and now I could barely get out of bed. What did I have to offer them in that state? I told myself they were better off without me in their lives, at least for now. And I almost believed it. The part of me that did not believe, it was the part that was keeping me alive, even when I did not want to be kept.

I thought about taking my own life more than once during that time. I do not say this lightly or for effect. I say it because it is the truth, and I think the truth needs to be said out loud, especially for anyone who has ever found themselves in that same dark corridor, wondering whether anyone would notice the light going out. I was in that corridor. I stood in it for a long time. On some days, Leigh would come around, and I would drag myself out of bed to open the door. On other days, I would just lie there and listen to him knock until he gave up and went away. Those were the days when I had nothing left at all.

We held a small funeral for Wendy. Just close family. She was cremated and placed in the rose garden, with a large concrete angel that I painted myself. I painted it slowly, carefully, and I think that is the first thing I did in that period that felt like something other than pure survival. Putting colour onto something. Making something beautiful for her, even though she could not see it.

It was around this time that I discovered P!NK's music, and I say discovered deliberately, because it felt like a discovery, like finding something that had been made specifically for me without the maker knowing I existed. Her songs found every bruise I had inside and pressed on them in a way that somehow relieved the pressure rather than adding to it. When I was suicidal, her music would pull me back. Not always by making me feel better. Sometimes, by simply making me feel understood, that is often enough when you are at the bottom. You just need to know that someone else has been to the bottom too and climbed back up. Her songs told me that.

Then I found out I was pregnant again. Life has a way of continuing regardless of whether you are ready for it. Things between Leigh and me were stable on the surface, though I was not in love with him, and part of me had always known I would not be. He had taken us in. He had been there through Wendy. But there was a possessiveness in him that had begun to show itself in small, relentless ways. If I went to the supermarket wearing makeup, he would accuse me of meeting another man. If I did not answer the phone immediately, he would convince himself I had someone in the house. He needed to know where I was at every moment, and when I could not account for every moment, his imagination filled in the gaps with whatever was worst.

That kind of jealousy is exhausting in a way that is difficult to explain to someone who has not experienced it. It is not dramatic. It does not come with shouting all the time or visible bruises. It comes as a constant low-level pressure, a requirement to justify yourself that never ends, a slow erosion of the sense that you are allowed to simply exist without explanation. I was already fragile. I was already carrying more grief than I knew what to do with. And now I was also being monitored.

After our daughter Bridgette was born, I began the process of coming off methadone. My doctor had told me I needed to wait until after the birth, and I had waited. Now I was ready. I got myself down to 0.05 milligrams, and then I came off it entirely. I want to say something about that, because it is easy to write it as a single sentence and move on, but it was not a single sentence in my life. It was months of work, of discomfort, of choosing every day to do the hard thing instead of the easy thing. I did it because I wanted my children back. I did it because I had decided that wanting my children back was worth every difficulty that stood between me and that goal.

I worked with welfare. I did the parenting courses. I did the anger management class. I showed up when I was asked to show up, and I did the things I was asked to do, and slowly, over time, the picture began to change. My older children came home. Not overnight. Not in one fell swoop. Bit by bit, they came back to me, and each one felt like a piece of myself returning. They were in high school by the time it happened, which meant I had lost years with them that I would never get back. That grief sits alongside the others. I do not dwell in it, but I do not pretend it is not there.

Leigh's abuse became physical on a number of occasions. He would hit me, mostly when I would not drink with him. I gave him fifty percent custody of Bridgette because, at the time, I genuinely believed he was a good father, and that belief was important enough to me to override what I knew about who he was to me as a partner. I wanted Bridgette to have her dad. I wanted to do the right thing by her, even at a cost to myself.

But cracks began to appear. On the nights when Bridgette was at her father's house, I would sometimes see Leigh's car parked outside my place in the dark. Watching. He was going through my rubbish bins to see what I had been eating, what I had been buying, and who might have been at my house. He rang welfare and told them I was back on drugs. Welfare took Bridgette from me for two weeks while I completed a series of urine tests. I submitted to every test. Every single one came back clean. They returned her to me. But those two weeks cost me something I cannot name. The humiliation of being disbelieved. The terror of losing her. The rage at the man who had set it all in motion.

One night, Bridgette started crying and told me she did not want to go to her father's. The next morning, she paced the kitchen, begging me not to send her. I sat down with her. I asked her what was happening. She told me her father had thrown a cup of coffee at her and that he had thrown a lunchbox lid at her. He told her regularly not to sleep in my bed because when she was at his place, I had different men in the house. She was a child. He was filling her head with that. I did not send her back. Leigh got lawyers to write me letters, but I did not send them back. There are things a mother will not do, regardless of legal pressure, and sending my daughter back to a house where she was being frightened and lied to was one of them.

By this point, I had been working at K&D Cafe as a cook, and I had also gotten my daughter, Charlene, a job there. We had built ourselves a small, good life around that work. On Friday nights, a group of us from work would go out together. It felt normal. It felt like something ordinary people did, and I had not had many ordinary things in my life for a long time.

One of those nights, we were at the *Queens Head Hotel*. Charlene, my boss, a couple of the other girls from work, and I. We were dancing. I was on the dance floor, feeling like a person rather than a problem, when I spotted Leigh standing in the crowd. Just standing there. Watching me. I felt the familiar cold shift in my stomach that his presence always caused. I said to Charlene that we should leave. We went back to the bar, then slipped out and started walking into town. Leigh followed.

We made it to another nightclub and thought we had lost him. We were dancing when I ran into an old friend from school. We hugged. We kissed each other on the cheek, the way old friends do. And then I felt a blow to the side of my head. Leigh had come from nowhere and hit me with his glass. The alcohol spilled over me. He was shouting. I stood there for a moment, getting my balance back, and I made the decision I almost always made with violent men: I chose to leave rather than escalate. I told Charlene we were going home.

We took a taxi back. Just as we were getting out, Leigh pulled up in his own taxi behind us. We ran inside and locked the door. He pounded on it. After a while, we thought he had gone. Charlene went outside for a cigarette. I went with her. And then we saw him run out from my carport. We saw the flames. He had set Charlene's car on fire.

I grabbed the hose. I tried to put it out. The water made it worse. I was in a conjoined unit, which meant the fire was moving toward the neighbouring home. While Charlene called the fire brigade, I ran to the neighbour's door and hammered on it until they woke up and got out. The fire engines came. The police came. We gave our statements. Leigh was charged. It made the newspaper, a piece in the Mercury about what he had done. I read it with something between satisfaction and disbelief. It was in print. It was real. He had finally done something public enough that the world could see it.

After everything, I kept working. I kept building. I saved every spare dollar I had, quietly and deliberately, the way you save when you know exactly what you are saving for. The *One Direction* concert in Melbourne. Bridgette had talked about it the way only a young girl can talk about something she loves completely, with her whole body, eyes wide, words tumbling over each other. I listened to her talk about it, and I made myself a quiet promise.

When the day finally came, I think I was as excited as she was, maybe more. We flew to Melbourne together, just the two of us, and there was something about that, about it being just us, that made it feel sacred. No chaos. No looking over our shoulders. No one we had to be afraid of. Just me and my girl on an adventure that I had made happen with my own two hands and my own hard work.

I watched her get ready that night, and I had to stop myself from crying. She was so happy. That particular happiness that belongs only to children at the thing they have been waiting for, pure and uncomplicated and absolutely glowing. She knew every word to every song. She sang them at the top of her lungs without embarrassment, without holding anything back, and I stood next to her and sang too, badly, and she laughed at me, and I did not care even slightly.

When the lights went down, and the crowd screamed, and the music started, I looked at her face. Just her face. And I thought: this is it. This is what I have been fighting for. Not just survival. Not just getting through one more day without falling apart. But in this exact moment, her joy, her safety, her hand finding mine in the dark because she wanted to share it with me. The fact that I was the one who brought her here. That I had worked and saved and held myself together long enough to give her this one perfect night.

I have had a lot of hard memories in my life. But I have that one too. And nobody can take it from me.

I got a job at the University of Tasmania. I got my daughter Stephanie a job there, too. We did catering work for different departments. We took a family holiday to Queensland together. These things might sound small to someone who has not had to fight for them, but to me, they were enormous. They were proof that I had come through. Not unscathed. Never unscathed. But through.

Eventually, because Leigh continued to hover around the unit where Bridgette and I were living, watching us, making the air feel unsafe, we moved to Glenorchy. A new place. A new start. Another beginning in a long line of beginnings. I have had to begin more times than I can count, and each time it has cost me something. But I am still here. I am still beginning.

There is a rose garden with a concrete angel in it that I painted with my own hands. Wendy is there. She will always be there. And every time I have thought about giving up, every time the dark has come in too close and I have stood at the edge of it, wondering whether to step over, I have thought about her. About all of them. About what it means to still be breathing when you have had every reason to stop.

CHAPTER 12:
HAPPY ON MY OWN

Bridgette and I had been living in Glenorchy for a while by this point. My older children had all moved into their own places. They had partners. Some of them had children of their own. I was a grandmother, and I loved being a grandmother in a way I had not expected to love it. There is something about grandchildren that feels like a second chance, not to redo the past, but to enjoy the present without carrying quite so much fear. I could watch them grow, learn, and make noise without the constant terror that someone was going to come through the door and shatter everything. That particular terror had finally started to quiet down, at least most days.

Bridgette was in high school. She was growing up, becoming her own person, and I was trying to give her the space to do that while also staying close enough that she knew I was there. It was a balance I was still learning. Sometimes she would decide she wanted to see her father, Leigh. Not often. But sometimes. I would drop her off at his place when she asked, and I never said no, even though part of me wanted to. She needed to make her own choices about him, and I respected that. But she was never there long. Within an hour, sometimes less, my phone would light up with a text from her asking me to come pick her up. Dad was carrying on again. That was how she would put it, and I knew exactly what she meant. I would drive over and collect her, and we would go home, and that would be that.

Leigh was still calling welfare on me. Still making things up, still trying to cause trouble in whatever way he could manage from a distance. They would ring me. I would talk to them.

Everything would be fine. They did a home visit to the Glenorchy house at one point, and I remember using that visit to ask them a question that had been sitting on my mind for weeks. I had just been offered a job at Wrest Point Casino as a cook. The job had not started yet. I had two weeks before my first shift. But some of the shifts were nights, and I wanted to make sure that was allowed, that I was not going to get in trouble for leaving Bridgette alone in the evening while I worked.

The welfare workers spoke to Bridgette directly. They asked her how she felt about me working night shifts. She told them she was fine with it, that she was old enough to be home on her own, that she could call me anytime if she needed me. They said it was okay for me to take the job. I also made sure Bridgette knew she could ring me at any point during my shift, and I asked my neighbours to keep an eye on her as well. When I started the night shifts, I would call Bridgette multiple times throughout the evening just to check in. I always told her to ring me before she went to bed, and she always did. Things were going well. We had found a rhythm that worked for both of us.

We had our mother-daughter date night once a week. We would go out for tea, just the two of us, and talk about whatever was on her mind. We also spent time with my grandchildren whenever we could, and I loved every minute of it. My days and nights were full in a good way, the kind of full that feels like purpose rather than chaos. Some nights we would be sitting on the couch watching a movie together when my phone would light up with a text from Leigh saying something like, "Why is Bridgette at the Sun Valley? I just saw her." It was a lie. Bridgette would be sitting right beside me. I stopped answering those messages. There was no point. If I responded, it would just go back and forth endlessly, and I had learned by now that engaging with Leigh's accusations only fed them. I would simply turn to Bridgette and say, "Your father is carrying on again," and she would roll her eyes and say, "Oh God, again." We had our own shorthand for it by then.

I know people reading this might be thinking, why did you not just change your phone number? The answer is simple, even if it is complicated. If Leigh did not have my number and something happened to Bridgette while she was with him, he would have no way to contact me. I needed that line open, even if it meant enduring his harassment. It was the cost of making sure my daughter was safe, and I was willing to pay it.

I was single for probably the first time in my adult life. At first, I was scared to be alone. I would sleep with multiple lights on in the house. Sometimes I would leave the television on just to have the sound of voices filling the space. I had been led to believe, for most of my life, that you had to be with a man to be happy. I had wanted so badly to be in love and to have someone love me back the way I loved them. But that had not happened for me, not in the way I had hoped it would. And at some point during those early months of being on my own, I started to ask myself why any man would love me when I felt like my own parents could not. I started to think that maybe there was something fundamentally wrong with me, something unlovable baked into who I was.

But there was one thing I knew for sure, and it was this: I was tired of being a punching bag. I was exhausted by the cycle of hoping someone would be different and then discovering they were not. I was done. So I stayed single. I concentrated on Bridgette. I concentrated on my adult children and my grandchildren. Whenever I felt low or depressed, I had my music. P!NK's songs had become a kind of anchor for me, something I could return to when the loneliness felt too heavy. And when

Bridgette would stay at her friends' houses and the silence in my home became too loud, I would visit my best mate, Nat.

Nat had become a big part of my life. He was the kind of friend you could talk to about anything without fear of judgement, and that kind of friendship is rare. I could tell him things I could not tell anyone else, and he would just listen. He never tried to fix me or tell me what I should do. He just heard me. That was enough. When I was tired of being stuck in the house, and Bridgette was busy with her own friends, Nat and I would go out for lunch or just hang out together. He was like a big brother to me, steady and safe, and I valued that more than I can say. Bridgette and I had built a routine in our lives, and for the first time in a very long time, that routine felt sustainable. It felt like something I could keep doing without it all falling apart.

Then, P!NK announced she was doing a concert in Melbourne. I thought about it for a few days. Should I go? Could I afford it? Was it worth it? And then I realised something that felt almost revolutionary at the time: I did not have to ask anyone for permission. If I wanted to go, I could just go. I would take Bridgette. We could turn it into a shopping trip as well, make a whole weekend out of it. Once the tickets went on sale, I got there an hour early. I was the second person in line at Bellerive to purchase the tickets, and I was so excited I could hardly stand still. But even after I had the tickets in my hand, it still did not feel entirely real.

I booked our flights. I booked the hotel room. It was still a few months away, and the waiting felt endless. Bridgette was excited, but not as excited as I was. I do not think she understood what this meant to me yet. When we finally arrived in Melbourne, we took the shuttle bus to the hotel and slept that first night. The next morning, we went to the markets and had an absolutely brilliant time, just wandering and looking at things and being together. That night we got ready and went to the concert. We took our seats. We were right in front of the stage. It was perfect.

Then the lights went down. P!NK came out. And before she even started singing, I started to cry. Not just a few tears. I was sobbing and laughing at the same time, and I could not stop. Bridgette looked at me and asked why I was crying. I could not answer her at that moment because I did not have the words yet. But I know now, looking back, what was happening. I felt freedom. That sounds corny to some people, I am sure. It might even sound silly. But I had so many emotions hitting me all at once, and freedom was at the centre of all of them.

I was not ruled by anyone anymore. I was not anyone's punching bag. I did not have to ask permission to spend my own money. I did not have to walk around my home on eggshells, waiting for the next explosion. All of those emotions hit me like a brick wall, and underneath all of them was something I had not felt in years: happiness. Not relief. Not survival. Actual happiness. I was happy just being me, not changing for anyone, not shrinking myself to fit into someone else's idea of who I should be. I was myself, and I was starting to like that person. That is why I was crying. Some people will not understand that, and some will. But it was one of the most powerful moments of my life.

After we spent a few days in Melbourne, we went home. I went back to work. Bridgette went back to school. Our lives went on. And somewhere in all of that, I came to a decision that felt both sad and peaceful at the same time: I would probably be on my own forever, and I was okay with that. I had tried love. I had tried relationships. They had not worked out for me in the way I had hoped. But I had my children. I had my grandchildren. I had my work, my music, and my friend Nat. I had a life that was mine, and that was enough.

The next part of this story is difficult to write because it involves my daughter in a way that feels like it crosses into her privacy. Bridgette became pregnant while she was in high school. I am not going to go into detail about who the father was, or how it happened, or what the circumstances were. That is not my story to tell. It is hers, and she deserves to tell it herself if and when she chooses to. But I will talk about the birth of her baby and how I felt, because that is my story, and it is part of this chapter of my life.

I supported my daughter and her decision. I was still working at Wrest Point at the time. I set my bedroom up as a nursery and moved myself into the lounge room. I did not think twice about it. Bridgette needed the space, and I could sleep anywhere. Eventually, I had to give up work entirely. One night, I came home from a shift and walked in the front door, and I could hear Bridgette vomiting. I rushed into her room. She was asleep and vomiting at the same time, and I have no idea how she did not wake up. The sound of it, the sight of it, scared me in a way I cannot fully describe. After that night, I was too frightened to go to work. I tried a few more times. I told Bridgette to prop herself up in bed before falling asleep, hoping that would help. But the fear became too much. I stopped working so I could be home with her. She needed me more than I needed the job.

When Bridgette went over her due date, the hospital booked her in to be induced. They put the drip in, and we just had to wait. After a few hours, the nurse came in. Bridgette was in pain, but the nurse said things were not progressing as quickly as they would have liked. Bridgette was in a lot of pain. The doctor came around and offered her an epidural. They tried the first time. The doctor could not get the needle in. She tried again. Bridgette was in so much pain, and the doctor still could not get the needle in. They decided to wait. They checked the baby's heartbeat. They said the baby was distressed, and so was Bridgette. They thought it was best to do a caesarean section.

Everything started happening very fast. Everyone was running around. On the way to the theatre, I was holding Bridgette's hand. In the operating theatre, they checked the baby's heartbeat again. It was strong. And then it was not. They could not find the heartbeat anymore. It had stopped. I could feel the tears welling up in my eyes, and I was fighting them back with everything I had. Bridgette asked me what was wrong. I could not tell her. I lied and said everything was fine. But in my own heart, I did not know if that was true. I did not know anything in that moment except that I was terrified.

Bridgette was on the operating table, still holding my hand. They were prepping her for surgery. She was shaking so much that she was nearly coming off the table. The doctor told the nurses to hold her down. They started prepping her stomach. I was still fighting back the tears because she needed me to be strong for her. Then, finally, they put Bridgette to sleep. I left the room. I went back to her hospital room and waited. I could not help but think: what if her baby does not make it? How will Bridgette cope? And then the thought that was even worse: what if Bridgette does not make it? All of these fears came flooding in, and with them came the memory of losing Wendy. All of those emotions, all of that grief, came rushing back, and I had no control over any of it. I was so scared.

I paced that hospital room for hours. Hours felt like days. I kept asking for updates, and they kept saying she was still in theatre. Then at last she was in the recovery room. I asked them if the baby was okay. They said they could not tell me anything. I prepared myself for the worst. I had to push my own feelings aside because I knew I had to be strong for Bridgette, especially if she had lost her baby. I knew how hard that was going to be.

Then at last I was allowed to go to her. I walked into the room. She was awake. But there was no baby in the room. I was fighting back tears again as I went over and held her hand. She asked me where her baby was. I said the nurse should be in soon. And then the nurse walked in. She came over to Bridgette, and the first words out of her mouth were, "Your baby's heartbeat stopped." My eyes were filling up again. Before she even finished the sentence, I was already bracing for the worst. But then she kept talking: "Your baby's heartbeat stopped, but she is a fighter, and the doctor is still with her. We will bring her in soon."

I could no longer hold the tears in. They fell down my face, and I did not care. I thought, thank God. Thank God. My granddaughter had survived. She had fought her way back. And Bridgette was okay. We were all okay.

That is all I am going to share about Bridgette and my granddaughter, Savannah, out of respect for my daughter. The rest of that story is hers to tell if she wants to. But I will say that later on, Bridgette and Savannah moved into Small Steps, a supported housing unit where other young mums around Bridgette's age were also living. I continued to support them in every way I could. They would come home and stay two nights a week. The rest of the time, I was home alone.

During the days, I would have different grandchildren over. But the nights became very lonely. Whenever I felt depressed, I had my P!NK music, and it helped. But for the first time in my life, I was truly alone. The house was empty. Most people would probably love having the place to themselves, but I hated it. My children were all getting on with their lives, and I was happy for them. I was proud of them. But I was lonely, and it was not their job to keep me company, even though some of them tried.

It was during this time that I got a friend request on Facebook from Peter. I knew Peter from high school. We started chatting online, and it was good. Easy. We would catch up a couple of times a week for coffee or lunch, and I made it very clear to him from the beginning that I would never live with a man again. My home was my safe place, and I was not giving that up for anyone. He said he was okay with that. We started seeing more and more of each other over time, but we always planned when we would meet up next because I was pretty busy during the week helping Bridgette and Savannah. Once Bridgette got her own home through government housing, I helped her set it up. I helped her get the things that she and Savannah needed. My days were full.

But after a while, Peter started just turning up at my home when we had not made plans. At first, I did not really like that, but instead of telling him, I just let it go. I know I should have said something. I was not good at setting boundaries yet, not with men, and old habits die hard.

I was planning to go on another holiday. I asked Peter if he wanted to come with me. All of my children had their own plans, and I did not want to go alone. He said yes. I paid for everything: the flights, the hotel, all of it. On the day we were meant to leave, I met Peter at the airport. His mother had dropped him off. While we were waiting for the plane, Peter looked smashed off his head. I asked him what was wrong. He told me he had not gotten much sleep the night before. I accepted that. I had no reason to doubt him. On the plane, he could hardly keep his head up or his eyes open. I asked him again if he was sure he was not on anything. He said again that he was just tired. He slept the entire flight. I could not help but think that he was off his head, but I did not have proof, and I wanted to believe him.

Once we arrived at the hotel, we went straight to bed. The next morning, we went out, but Peter still seemed very sleepy. All he wanted to do was go to the pub. I told him I did not come all this way just to sit in a pub. He did not want to do anything else. I was determined to enjoy myself on this trip and do all the things I wanted to do, so I told him he could go to the pub on his own, and I would go do what I wanted. He went to the pub. I told him I would meet him back at the hotel later. I went off and did the things I had come to do, and I had a wonderful time on my own.

When I got back to the hotel, I did not think Peter was back yet. I walked into the bathroom to use the toilet, and my heart dropped. There was Peter with a 20 mil syringe, injecting himself with methadone. How could I have been so stupid? The words that came out of my mouth were just, "Why?" He tried to tell me it was okay, that it was not a big deal. It was not okay with me. It was the opposite of okay. I wanted to leave, but I could not. We were stuck there together for the rest of the trip. I told him to stay in the lounge room. I wanted nothing to do with any of this. It did not seem to bother him at all. All I could think was: how could I have been so stupid? I should have trusted my gut feeling at the airport.

The next day, I would get up and leave before he woke up, or while he was still passed out in the lounge chair. I would go out and enjoy my day on my own, wishing the entire time that I had just come by myself in the first place. The five days went fast. Then Peter ran out of methadone. He started drinking top-shelf spirits instead. The night before we had to leave to go home, I had been out all day, which is what I did every day to get away from Peter. When I got back to the hotel, Peter was not there. But he had put a post up on Facebook showing two bottles of top-shelf alcohol. My heart sank, and I started to feel scared.

Not long after, Peter walked through the door with one of the bottles in his hand, half full. I got up and said goodnight. I told him I was going to bed. I went into the bedroom. There was no lock on the door. I put a chair against it so that if I fell asleep and he tried to open it, the chair would fall over and make a noise and wake me up. I lay in bed praying for it to be morning. Peter was shouting at me from the lounge room. Then after a while, *bang*. The chair fell. Peter had come into the bedroom demanding to know why I did not want to be with him. I told him I did not want to be with anyone on drugs. He started abusing me, calling me fat and ugly, telling me I did not deserve to be with someone like him. He said he was too good for trash like me. I agreed with him, hoping he would leave me alone. He did not.

He had a knife. He would throw it at me, and it would hit the bedhead. I would move. He would grab it again. He held the knife to my throat and asked me if I thought I was better than him. I said no. I was terrified. I vomited all over myself from fear. He told me to get in the bathroom and clean myself up. I did. I was too scared to get changed. I just wiped the vomit off with toilet paper. Peter went back into the lounge room. I ran back into the bedroom and out on the balcony. I threw my bags over the edge. It made a loud noise. I was trying to figure out how to climb down to the balcony below to get away from Peter. I had one leg over the railing when Peter grabbed me by the hair and dragged me back into the room.

I sat on the bed crying, begging him to leave me alone. He did not. I did not sleep at all that night. Peter sat on the chair at the end of my bed. Whenever I thought he was asleep and I tried to leave, he would wake up. That morning, we left for the airport. Peter was still abusing me in the car on the way there. He even hit me in the side of the face while I was driving. I was so glad once we got to the airport. I was still crying, and the abuse did not stop. One of the workers came over and asked me if I was okay. Peter told her to fuck off, or she would cop it too. She left. She sent another worker over, a male worker this time. He helped me check in and put my bags through. Peter said nothing to him. I thanked him. I was waiting to board the plane when Peter disappeared.

We were boarding the plane, and Peter was nowhere to be seen. I rang his mother and asked her to ring him because he was about to miss the plane. I did not want to be responsible for him missing his flight and getting stranded. After all, I had brought him here. It felt like the right thing to do to make sure he got home. Peter made the plane at the last minute. I had to sit next to him. I was at the window seat, and I just kept looking out, trying to disappear into myself. Peter sat near me, still abusing me, still calling me names. The air hostess came around and asked if we wanted a snack. I said no thanks. Tears were running down my face. My face was red. Peter looked at her and said, "Does it look like she needs anything to eat? She is a fat pig." I did not say anything. Then two flight attendants came back and asked me if I was okay, if there was anything they could do. I said no, I was fine. I just wanted to get home.

Once the plane landed, before we got off, Peter tried to say sorry. He said he loved me. I said it was okay, not to worry about it. I was telling him what he wanted to hear so he would leave me alone. As soon as we got off the plane, I collected my bags. Peter collected his. He asked me to watch his bags while he went to the toilet. I said yes. And as soon as he was out of sight, I took off. I left his bags there and went straight outside and jumped into a taxi. Before I even got out of the airport car park, Peter was ringing me. I answered. I told him I was done. He asked how he was supposed to get home. I told him to ring his mother. Then I hung up. He tried ringing me many times after that. I did not answer.

After a few weeks, Peter started showing up at my house uninvited. I would never let him in. He would stand outside my front door, saying it was the methadone that made him act like that, that he had been double-dosing. I did not care. I was not going to give him another chance. I wanted better for myself. I was not going backwards. Then one day, he broke in through my back sliding door. He had a bottle of beer in his hand. I told him to get out. He kept saying he loved me, that he was sorry. He would not leave. So I walked out the back. He followed. He started pushing me. I kept telling him to fuck off. Then I heard the smash of the beer bottle. I turned around just as he swiped the broken bottle across my neck, cutting it. It started to bleed. Not spurting blood, but bleeding.

Someone had called the police. They asked me what had happened. Peter was standing right there. I was too scared to say anything, so I said I had done it to myself. They called an ambulance, and I went to the hospital. I was hoping the police would come to the hospital so I could tell them the truth, but they did not. I was so angry with myself for not telling them. I refused to go back to being that scared woman who was frightened of her own shadow. I made a promise to myself that I would never let a man treat me like this again.

After a few weeks, Peter started sending me threats. Pictures of a gun. Pictures of bullets. I was not going to take this type of abuse anymore. I went to the police station. I told them about the threats he had made. I showed them the messages. And I told them the truth about what had happened to my neck. I told them I just wanted him to leave me alone. They put a domestic violence order on him. He was not allowed to contact me or come anywhere near me.

I had learned something important through all of this. I had learned that I could survive on my own. That I did not need a man to complete me or make me feel whole. I had learned that loneliness was hard, but it was not as hard as living in fear. And I had learned that I was stronger than I had ever given myself credit for. I was still standing. I was still here. And I was not going to let anyone take that away from me again.

ZJ and his Sister Jaydah

ZJ and His Sister Indii

Poppy Darren with ZJ

CHAPTER 13:
PROTECTING MY GRANDSON AT ALL COSTS

One night, I was rushed to the hospital with chest pain and exhaustion so deep it felt like my body was shutting down. It was near Christmas, and I had convinced myself that I had simply overdone it with all the shopping I had to do. I thought I just needed rest. But the hospital found something else. They told me I had a heart condition called atrial fibrillation, where your heart beats too fast, and the rhythm is all wrong. Once they worked out what medication I needed, I was sent home. I was in the hospital for about a week.

At this time, my son James was in jail for driving offences. I did not go into detail about what was wrong with me when I spoke to my children. I told them I was fine. I did not want them worrying about me, and I did not want to be a burden. That is a pattern I have carried my whole life, this belief that my pain is something I should handle alone, that asking for help or admitting I am struggling makes me a problem rather than a person. So, I kept it to myself. I was fine. That is what I told everyone, even when I was not fine at all.

James had moved back home before all of this happened. His relationship with Sammy had broken down again, which did not surprise me in the slightest. I thought it was a strange relationship from the start. They were always on and off, seeing other people one day and back together the next. It was chaotic and unstable, and as far as I could see, it was a relationship built around drugs. They would be using meth one day, fine the next, then arguing, then using again. The cycle never stopped. When they separated this time, I felt a quiet relief. I was glad they had split up, honestly, because I could see what that relationship was doing to my son.

There were so many red flags about Sammy that I could not ignore. I saw the way she would treat her young daughter when she was coming down from drugs. I saw how, in the first couple of nights she and James got together, she would let James take her daughter without really knowing whether he was safe to be around a child. Now, I knew James was fine with the little girl, but how could Sammy have known that? She barely knew him. And sometimes when James had Sammy's daughter, Sammy would go on her drug binges, and we would not be able to get hold of her for days, sometimes weeks. Sometimes Sammy's family members would call James because they had her daughter and could not get hold of Sammy either. It was neglect, plain and simple, and I hated watching it unfold.

Once James was out of jail, he returned home to my place. I did not mind. I enjoyed having him there. We got on well, and I wanted to support him. I knew James had a drug problem, and he knew it too. The difference this time was that he wanted to get clean. He wanted help. I supported him in every way I could. I took him to the drug and alcohol services to get medication that would help him stay off the meth. I took him to counselling sessions. I sat with him through the hard days. It is not easy watching someone you love go through the ups and downs of addiction. I know how hard it is from my own experience with methadone. But James wanted to get clean, and I was determined to help him in any way I could.

Then Sammy started coming around again. I was not happy about it, but I could not tell my son who he could and could not see. James's recovery took a back seat. He would go over to Sammy's place and stay for days, sometimes longer, and when he came back, I would try to feed him up because I could tell he was back on the meth. I am not slamming Sammy here. James can make his own decisions. But whenever those two were together, it was all about the drugs. That was the sad truth of it.

Their relationship was on and off for a while. Then one night, when I thought they were truly over, James came into the lounge room and asked if it was okay for Sammy and her daughter to stay the night. I asked him why. He told me that Sammy's ex-partner, Jordan, had shot a gun off inside her place, and she was too scared to stay there. I said yes, of course, she could stay. The next day, Sammy left to go to her place to get some clothes. Her daughter stayed at home with James and me. It was then that James told me Sammy was pregnant and that he was the father.

I asked him how he could be sure he was the father; given that they had been broken up. He told me they had been seeing each other here and there without telling me, and that the timing worked out. I said, 'Oh, okay.' What else could I say? Sammy stayed another night, and then things went back to the way they normally were with those two. Drugs. On and off. On and off. Sammy was the type of person who would do anything for drugs, and that became very clear very quickly. One night, she came to our home at all hours of the morning. She had drugs with her. She told James she had slept with a guy down in Rokeby, so she would not have to pay for them. I heard them arguing and went in to see what was happening. James told me what she had said. Sammy sat there and did not say much. She ended up leaving, and they stopped seeing each other for a while.

Then James went back to jail on more driving charges. I bought clothes and toys for his and Sammy's baby. Sammy asked me if I wanted to be in the hospital when she gave birth. I told her I would love to be there, and I asked if I could film it for James so he could see his son being born, even if he could not be there in person. She said yes. So on the third of February 2024, I was in the hospital while Sammy was giving birth to my grandson. I filmed it for James. She gave birth to a little boy. Sammy's mum was also there. When I got to hold my grandson, ZJ James Duggan, I felt an overwhelming wave of love and also sadness. I felt sorry for my son, missing out on seeing his son being born. I held ZJ tight, and I could not help but feel a bit sorry for him as well. His mum was still on meth. His dad was in jail. He was coming into the world already at a disadvantage, and it broke my heart.

About three days after ZJ was born, Sammy asked me to watch him while she went shopping and to the pokies. She never came back that night. I did not mind. Then the next night, still no Sammy. I had to buy baby milk and nappies because she had not left enough. I tried calling her, but she would not answer. As I said, I did not mind, because I knew ZJ was safe with me. Sadly, Sammy was on one of her drug binges again. After about a week, she came and collected ZJ, but then she brought him back the next day. I would never refuse to have him. I could see her struggling, and more importantly, I could see that ZJ needed someone stable. She would collect him the next day, and then later that same day, she would ask me over to her place.

When I got there, she was giving ZJ Panadol because, as she said, he would not stop crying. Then her daughter asked for some, and Sammy gave her some as well. Not because the little girl needed it, but because she wanted it. That made my stomach turn. I took ZJ home with me that day. When James got out of jail, Sammy would stay at our home with both her children. Then one night, I woke up to ZJ screaming. I waited a few minutes because I did not want to go into the room where James, Sammy, and the children were sleeping. I did not want Sammy to feel like I was taking over or stepping on her toes as a mother. But ZJ's crying became too much for me to ignore. I went into the room. James was not there. Sammy was in bed with ZJ, and he was near the edge of the bed. I moved him to a safer spot, woke Sammy up, and told her the baby had been crying. She looked at me and said, 'I know.' I said, 'Well, fix him.' I walked out of the bedroom and into the kitchen to get myself a drink. James was asleep on the lounge. Sammy came out and got ZJ a bottle.

About ten minutes passed, and then I heard ZJ crying again. I went back into the bedroom. Sammy was in bed, asleep. She had put ZJ in his bouncer with his bottle and a blanket propped under the bottle to hold it up to his mouth. This made me so angry. A baby could choke like that. A baby could aspirate. I picked him up, took him into my room, got his wind up, fed him his bottle properly, changed his nappy, and put him back to sleep. Sammy left ZJ with me the next morning. For weeks after that, every now and then, she would show up at ridiculous times, demanding that I give ZJ to her. She was always on meth. I could just always talk her down, convince her not to take ZJ out in the cold or in the state she was in. Sometimes she would even stay the night, but by the time I got up at seven, she would be gone. ZJ would be left behind.

I tried to call Sammy on a number of occasions because ZJ's needles were due, and I did not want to take him without his parents' permission. But because I could not get hold of Sammy, I asked James. He said it was okay, that ZJ needed these immunisations. I did not want them to feel like I was taking over, but James asked me to step in and help with ZJ because he knew he could not do it on his own, and Sammy was all over the place. I agreed to do this for ZJ's sake. Sammy's mother was not doing anything to help. She does not really like to get involved, as far as I have seen, and she will just agree with whatever Sammy wants. Sadly, she will not say when her daughter is doing the wrong thing.

I had ZJ in my care for about eight months. I paid for everything for him. I did not go to Centrelink to get a payment for him because I thought if I did, Sammy would kick up a fuss about it, and I was happy to have ZJ as long as I knew he was safe. He is such a bundle of joy to have. I did not mind the sleepless nights. His safety was the most important thing to me. Nothing else mattered.

I had started talking to Darren on Facebook not long after ZJ was born. He had met my adult children, and he treated them with such respect. He had also met some of my grandchildren, including ZJ. He was very patient with me. He knew that ZJ was my main focus and that I had to be there for him. He understood this, which at first surprised me. My main focus was on ZJ. He needed me. My other grandchildren were okay with their parents. I had no fear of them, and I still saw them regularly. But ZJ was different. ZJ needed protecting.

Darren does not have children, so his patience and understanding with ZJ were something I valued deeply. I told him everything that was going on. I told him I needed to be there for ZJ no matter what. He understood. And when I say he understood, I mean he really did. At any time, if we were meant to catch up and I had to pull out at the last minute, or if I was a few hours late and I explained why, he was okay with it. Some nights, Darren would stay over, and some nights, if I was up and down with ZJ, Darren understood. The sleepless nights did not bother him. He got it. I found myself really falling for him, but I had to put the brakes on because ZJ was my main focus, and I did not want anything to interfere with that.

Then one day, I had just settled ZJ in the lounge room. I was in James's room talking to him when I heard a car beeping outside. At first I thought it was coming from James's TV, but then I realised it was coming from the street. I went outside to see what was going on. I noticed Sammy in the middle of the street in her car, yelling, 'Bring my son out, you swearing at me!' She was high on meth again. I told her to piss off. She screamed out, 'I will fucking kill you!' She yelled this three times, then drove off, shouting, 'We will be back!' I did not think I would hear from her for at least the rest of the night.

James left to go get smokes. Not long after, I could hear a car revving in my carport. Sammy was back. I thought I would try to go out and talk to her, to settle things down. ZJ was still asleep in the lounge room. I walked out my front door and started walking over to the driver's side of Sammy's car. Then Jordan, Sammy's ex-partner, who she had a no-contact order against, got out of the car and said, 'Go get him, slut.' He raised his hand, and I saw a gun. I recognised it. I had seen it before at Sammy's place. I started to run toward my front door. There was a bang and a smell like someone had let a firecracker off. I got inside, locked the front door, and ran to the lounge room. I picked ZJ up because I was going to go out the back and over the back fence. Then James came back over the back fence. I told him what had happened. I called the police.

The police came. I gave my statement. They blocked off a few streets, and within about an hour, they had Sammy and Jordan in custody. The bullet from the gun had gone through the bedroom window and landed on the wall above ZJ's cot. Sammy knew that was ZJ's bedroom window. She knew exactly where her son slept, and she had brought a man with a gun to that window. That knowledge sits in me like a stone I cannot spit out.

While all of this was going on, Darren continued to come to my home and support me in any way he could. Where most people would have thought, 'Bugger that, I am not getting involved,' he chose to stay and support me. The shooting happened in the late afternoon. Physically, I was not injured, but mentally I suffered. I had panic attacks. I had nightmares. Once I was able to get to the doctor, I was told I was suffering from PTSD symptoms. Everything had changed for me. I had to be medicated just to stay in my own home. But one thing did not change: I would do whatever I could to protect my grandson.

My safety felt like it had been ripped away from me. I hated feeling so helpless, so scared at sudden noises. If I left my home, I made sure I had someone with me. The fear of being in my home became too much for me. My other grandchildren could not visit me because of the fear that Sammy and Jordan might come back at any time. I understood this. I would not put any of them at risk. I had to move to a new place where I have security cameras all around my home. Later on, Jordan pleaded guilty to the shooting. The gun had been made on a 3D printer. He went to jail.

At the end of all this, the family court awarded custody to Sammy, despite her failing a hair follicle test for drugs. They granted me one day a week and one night with ZJ. I was hoping that going through court, Sammy might have woken up to herself and gotten off drugs. Sadly, that is not the case. Today, she is back in court for what I believe are drug-related charges. One thing I know for sure is that I will never give up on ZJ's safety, and I will keep fighting for him no matter what.

I still talk to Nat on a daily basis, or every other day. We did talk about the shooting. I also talked to him about Darren. He even met Darren, and Nat's words were, 'About time you found someone decent. You deserve to be happy.' Darren and I are officially dating now. I did put us on hold for a while because I was only focusing on ZJ, and he understood and still hung around, which meant so much to me. At the time, Darren's friendship meant everything. I had never had a man who understood that he was not my main focus at that point. That kind of patience and understanding was new to me, and it was something I did not take for granted.

My P!NK music was still very important to me during all of this. I was still listening to it when I needed help just to get through the day. There are two songs by P!NK's that are my go-to songs, the ones that pull me up when I think I am losing myself again. Those songs are 'Nobody Knows' and 'Conversations with My 13-Year-Old Self.' These two songs pull me out of my darkest days. They remind me that I have survived before, and I can survive again. They remind me that I am still here, still standing, still fighting for the people I love.

This chapter of my life has been one of the hardest. Watching my son struggle with addiction. Watching my grandson come into the world, already surrounded by chaos. Being shot at in my own home. Developing PTSD. Moving house because I no longer felt safe. Fighting in court for the right to protect a child who needed protecting. These are not small things. These are the kinds of experiences that break people. But I am still here. I am still fighting. And as long as ZJ needs me, I will keep showing up. No matter what it costs me. No matter how hard it gets. That is what love looks like. That is what protection looks like. And I will never stop.

CHAPTER 14:
LOVE WITH NO STRINGS ATTACHED

I used to think I was unlovable. That belief sat in me like a stone I had swallowed years ago, something heavy and solid that I carried everywhere without really noticing the weight anymore. I used to live in my own head, turning the same thoughts over and over like prayer beads. How dare I expect anyone to truly love me when I felt like my own parents didn't? What right did I have to expect love when I was so obviously broken, when my body carried a lifetime of physical scars, and my mind carried even more scars that no one could see?

I had built invisible walls around myself to protect what was left of me. I had built them so high and so thick that even I could not see over them anymore. How could anyone get close to me when I had constructed my own fortress? And more to the point, why would anyone want to? I knew I was damaged. I knew I came with baggage that most people would not want to carry. I had convinced myself that love, real love, was something that happened to other people. Not to me. Never to me.

When I first met Darren, I did not expect it to go anywhere beyond friendship. I was not looking for love. In fact, I had given up on it entirely. The only experiences I had with love had been bad ones, painful ones, violent ones. If that was what love looked like, then I wanted no part of it. I was done. I had decided I would rather be alone than be hurt again, and I meant it.

At first, Darren would come around here and there. He would stay some nights and not others. On the nights he did stay, if my grandchildren were due to come over the next morning, I would make sure Darren was not there. I did not want them to see me with someone when I was not sure where things were going. I have granddaughters in high school, and I was conscious of what message I was sending them. ZJ was always at my home because he was still a baby, so he did not understand any of it. Darren also met my son James, because James lived with me at the time. The respect Darren showed James was beautiful. He treated him like a person, not like a problem or a burden. That meant something to me.

The way Darren would play and interact with ZJ was so beautiful and sweet. When ZJ would wake up during the night, it did not bother Darren at all. On the nights I would walk up and down my hallway trying to settle ZJ when he was teething, Darren would just lie there quietly, never once complaining, never once making me feel like I was an inconvenience. Darren would even offer to hold ZJ if I had to get him a bottle. This sort of thing was new to me. I had never experienced a man who saw a crying baby as something to help with rather than something to resent.

Even on nights when Darren was not at my place, when he would text me, he would always ask how ZJ was. I found this strange, not in a creepy way, but in a sweet way. I used to think to myself, who is this man? Why have I never met someone like this before? I must admit, at first I thought it must be a front. I thought he was putting on an act, that eventually the mask would slip and I would see who he really was underneath. But it was not a front. It was just him. I struggled with trusting that it was real, but it was. And as time went on, things stayed the same. He stayed the same. That consistency was something I had never experienced before.

I found myself falling for Darren quite quickly, which terrified me. I even tried to stop myself. My radar when it came to men had been so off in the past that I did not trust my own judgement anymore. I stopped seeing him so much during the week, thinking that distance would help me get perspective. But that only made me think of him more. I would find myself in my own head again, turning things over. I know he treats my son and grandson absolutely beautifully, I would think, but is that enough for me to give him a chance? And was this my chance to have love? I had given up on it. I had made peace with being alone. But here was this man, patient and kind, and I did not know what to do with that.

I had a lot going on at this time. My main focus was on ZJ and keeping him safe. So I pushed my feelings aside. I told myself that even if Darren was different, even if he was kind, I did not have the space in my life for a relationship. ZJ needed me. That had to come first. Everything else could wait.

Then the shooting happened at my home. I was meant to pick Darren up that night. James rang Darren and told him what was going on while I gave my statement to the police. I did not think I would see Darren after that. I thought that would be it, that he would decide I came with too much drama, too much danger, too much mess. But he still continued to come to my place. This shocked me. I kept thinking, why would he want to get involved with all this trouble? And there was a simple answer to that, even though it took me a while to accept it. Darren cared about us. It was that simple. But it was not simple for me at first. I kept playing it over in my mind. Why did he not just walk away?

Things were great between Darren and me. He knew my main focus was ZJ and doing what I had to do to keep him safe. I had lawyers' appointments and court hearings to attend. Darren even watched ZJ for me a couple of times while I attended these appointments. That kind of support was foreign to me. I was used to doing everything on my own, to being told I was on my own. Having someone step in without being asked, without complaining, without making me feel guilty for needing help, that was new. It was so new that I did not know how to receive it at first.

Then I let Darren meet my other adult children and my other grandchildren. I kept waiting and expecting things to fall apart between us. I kept bracing for the moment when he would show his true colours, when the kindness would run out, when the patience would wear thin. But that moment never came. I believe we just got stronger. And that confused me more than anything.

One day, I took Darren down to the supermarket. I sat in the car while he went in. He came out with groceries, and I remember asking him why he had gotten groceries for my place. He said, 'Well, I have been staying at your place here and there.' I did not really know what to say. I remember thinking to myself, who is this man? And who are his parents, because they have brought up a caring and loving person. I had never had someone do that for me before. It might seem like a little thing to some people, but it meant the world to me. It was not just about the groceries. It was about the fact that he saw himself as part of my life, that he contributed without being asked, that he did not keep a tally of what he gave versus what he got back.

Even if Darren was at home and paid for takeout, he would also pay for James as well. These small acts of kindness kept stacking up, and I did not know what to do with them. I was not used to generosity without strings. I was not used to being cared for in a way that felt genuine and uncomplicated.

I still spoke to my mate Nat on a daily basis during all of this. Nat had been my constant, my steady friend through so much, and I valued that friendship more than I can say. I also still had my P!NK music to pull me out of my darkest days. My go-to songs were 'Nobody Knows' and 'Conversations with My 13-Year-Old Self.' In the past, these songs had pulled me out of depression and times when I had been suicidal. They had pulled me back from the edge more times than I could count. But now, I was listening to P!NK music just to simply enjoy it and sing along. It still made me feel good, but it was different now. I was not using it to survive anymore. I was using it to live.

Then one day, after court, I was very emotional. Things just got on top of me, and I broke down crying. Darren did not judge me. He did not tell me to pull myself together or to be strong. He just simply gave me his shoulder to cry on, which was strange but nice at the same time. I was not used to having someone there like that for me. I was used to crying alone, to dealing with my emotions in private, to never letting anyone see me fall apart because showing weakness always seemed to invite more pain. But with Darren, it was different. He just let me cry. He did not try to fix it or rush me through it. He just held the space for me to feel what I was feeling.

I found myself leaning on Darren more when James went back to jail. When I noticed I was doing this, I would pull away from him. I did not want to rely on him. I did not want to need him. Because of my past experiences, I did not want to rely on a man ever again. I am strong. I can do things on my own. That is what I told myself. But Darren was there for us, and I battled with that in my own mind. I found it hard to accept that there was no hidden agenda. I kept waiting for the other shoe to drop, for him to use my dependence against me, to hold it over my head. But there was no hidden agenda. There never was.

I had to move to a new place after the shooting because I did not feel safe anymore. Darren rolled up his sleeves and helped me move with no hesitation. He did not complain. He did not make me feel like a burden. He just showed up and helped. That is who he was. That is who he is.

My relationship with Darren is strong, but I still battle with it in my head. I still ask myself questions that I know are rooted in fear rather than reality. Will this last? Will things change? Will he ever raise his hand to me? These are my insecurities, not Darren's actions. He has done nothing to make me have these thoughts. But they come anyway, uninvited, like ghosts from relationships past. I am learning to recognise them for what they are. I am learning to separate the past from the present. It is hard work, and some days are easier than others.

All my grandchildren call Darren 'Poppy' now. It is adorable. Darren is a very sweet and patient man, which is very new to me, and I like it. I more than like it. I need it. I deserve it. That is something I am learning to say to myself without feeling guilty.

We have had our disagreements about things. We cannot always be on the same page. But that is all they are: disagreements. I am not in fear of Darren hitting me simply because I do not agree with him on something. That might sound like a small thing, but it is everything. I can even leave a cup in the sink overnight, and I can stay in my pyjamas all day on a Sunday without the fear of Darren flying off the handle at me. I do not have to walk on eggshells in my own home anymore, and it feels great. It feels like freedom.

Darren has told me he loves me, and I believe he does. I love him too. I did not think I would ever find love. I was a broken person when I met Darren. I was healing slowly, and I still am. I never expected to find true love with no strings attached, but I have. Darren does not need me to change or be anyone other than myself for him to love me, and it is a bloody great feeling. He loves me as I am. Scars and all. Walls and all. Trauma and all. He does not try to fix me or save me. He just walks beside me while I do the work of fixing myself.

I have met Darren's family. I was scared to meet Darren's cousin Katie, but she made me feel very welcome in her home. I was also scared to meet Darren's mum, Karen. My own insecurities came flooding in. Would I be good enough for her son? Would she see all the ways I was broken and decide I was not worthy of him? All of those thoughts raced through my mind. But Darren's mum made it easy. It is hard to explain and put into words what she is like. If I had to describe her, I would say she is warm and loving. That is the best way I can put it.

Lately, Darren's mum and I have been spending time together, going out to lunch or shopping. She has even come to my home and stayed the night on a few different occasions, and I love every minute of it. At first, I was not sure if she would accept me. Again, my own insecurities were coming in. You hear different stories about mothers-in-law, and I had braced myself for the worst. But I have hit the jackpot. I have the best mother-in-law. We text each other a lot, and at the end of every text, she tells me she loves me. At first, I was not sure how to answer that. I was not used to anyone saying that to me, especially not a parental figure. She says it after every message. But now I simply answer her with 'I love you too,' because I do love her. She has shown me a kind of maternal warmth that I never had from my own mother, and it means more to me than I know how to express.

I feel very lucky. I am in love, and I am being loved the way I wanted to be all my life. I still have my invisible walls up, but Darren is helping me take them down slowly without even knowing it. He is not trying to knock them down or force his way through. He is just there, patient and steady, and somehow that makes it safe enough for me to start dismantling them myself, brick by brick.

I am learning what healthy love looks like. I am learning that love does not have to hurt. I am learning that being cared for does not mean being controlled. I am learning that a man can be strong without being violent, that he can be present without being possessive, that he can love me without needing to own me. These are lessons I never thought I would get to learn. I thought I had missed my chance. I thought I was too old, too damaged, too far gone. But I was wrong.

So after everything I have been through, my love did come. It came at a time I was not looking for it. It came at a time I had given up on it and was not expecting it. And it also came with no strings attached. That is the best part about it. There are no conditions. There is no fine print. There is just love, simple and honest and steady. The kind of love I used to think only existed in films or in other people's lives. But it exists in mine now, too. And I am learning, slowly, to believe that I deserve it. That I am worthy of it. That being broken does not mean being unlovable. It just means I have survived things that would have destroyed weaker people. And Darren sees that. He sees my strength, not just my scars. He sees who I am, not just what has been done to me. And that makes all the difference.

CHAPTER 15:
STILL STANDING

I hate most of my past. That is the truth, raw and unvarnished. I wish I could go back and change things, but sadly, we cannot rewrite what has already been written. Looking back now, I can see that I was just a scared little girl, too frightened to speak up for myself, always living in fear. But as much as I hate my past and wish things had been different, there are six things I have never, ever regretted. Those six things are my six beautiful children. They are a big part of why I survived. They are why my heart continues to beat today.

Sadly, in this world, people seem obsessed with labels and judgement instead of offering a helping hand. People will listen to rumours and judge you without even knowing your story. I have experienced this more times than I can count. I used to believe that if you treated people with love, understanding, and kindness, they would return it. But sadly, life taught me otherwise. People will be who they are. They will believe what they want and act however they choose, regardless of how it affects you. And that is on them, not on you. At the end of the day, I have learnt that actions speak the loudest and words often mean the least.

I believe today that not everyone is meant to grow or heal with you, and that is okay. Healing does happen, and it can change you. You learn to set boundaries. My own healing has taught me to stop tolerating chaos. It has taught me to walk away from negativity, even when it is uncomfortable, even when it involves people I love, like friends and family members. I know everyone's healing journey will be different. My healing journey required me to let go of the version of myself that overgave, over-explained, over-thought, and just stayed silent to keep others comfortable.

Choosing yourself is not betrayal. It is peace. And the people who truly belong in your life will not be threatened by your peace. They will respect it. I believe that every single year has shaped me into the woman I am today. The mistakes. The lessons. The heartbreak. The ups and the downs, more downs than I would have liked. The wins. The laughter and love. And sadly, the abuse I have suffered. I have used it all to build up strength in me.

There is something so freeing about healing and not feeling like you have to shrink yourself anymore or hide in the shadows so you are out of the way. No one gets to rewrite your story. Every choice you make, every risk you take, shapes who you are. Healing can feel like freedom. It feels like the world has been lifted from your shoulders.

All the abuse I suffered over the years, physical abuse, mental abuse, sexual abuse, and neglect, has not made me bitter. When really, I could have walked away from all of this as a very hateful person. But that is not me. I love to help and show love. I am not saying I have walked away from all this abuse without scars, because trust me, I have plenty. But I will not let it define me. It has been a very long journey to recovery, but I was not going to let what happened to me be my only story.

I tried counselling, and I would urge anyone suffering from abuse of any kind to reach out, as it may help. But sadly, for my healing journey, I felt it was not for me. So I turned to my P!NK music. She became my counsellor without even knowing it. P!NK's music touched me in a way that is hard to explain. We all need something or someone we can relate to. P!NK was it for me. She played a big part in my healing.

I will share a few moments of how she helped me. Whenever I would feel depressed, I would play her album 'I'm Not Dead.' I would sing, cry, and laugh, sometimes all at the same time. And by the end of the album, I would feel good again. P!NK's songs

'Nobody Knows' and 'Conversations with My 13 Year Old Self' have brought me back from my suicide thoughts. I hate to think what would have happened to me back then if I had not had my P!NK music, especially after the loss of my daughter Wendy.

I believe today I can honestly say P!NK saved my life, and I am so grateful for her music. Some people may say you had children, which is a reason not to give up, and that is true. But when you are travelling down that road of darkness and just want all the pain to stop, it is hard to see and think clearly. There were times I would find myself sitting in my car with a bottle of pills, trying to find the courage to end all my pain. And when you are in that state of mind, you do not think about anything other than ending your pain. When I found myself in these states, lucky for me, P!NK's CD with my two go-to songs was in my car stereo, and I guess she would bring me back to reality.

As I have said, today I listened to P!NK music simply to enjoy it. I have come a long way to get where I am today. I am not that scared little girl anymore. I can speak my mind and stand up and make sure I am heard, which is a great feeling. And I can stand up for those who do not have a voice yet, like my grandson.

People may ask why I am sharing all this. It is not for pity. Please do not pity me. It is simple. I am sharing because if anyone has suffered from any abuse, I want to show them there is a light at the end of the tunnel. It does take time, and we learn to be patient with ourselves. You can heal. We may not be able to change our past, but we can live our future the way we want.

Today I feel lucky to wake up and face another day, to love and laugh louder and hug my grandchildren tighter. I feel so blessed. It took me years to get to this point in my life, but I made it. And you can too. I feel free, and my life is full of love and happiness.

This is what survival looks like. It does not look like perfection. It does not look like never struggling or never feeling the weight of what came before. Survival looks like getting up one more time than you were knocked down. It looks like choosing yourself even when it feels selfish. It looks like setting boundaries with people you love. It looks like crying in your car to P!NK songs and then driving home to make dinner for your grandchildren. It looks like learning to trust again, even when every part of you wants to build higher walls. It looks like falling in love at a time you had given up on it. It looks like standing in your kitchen in your pyjamas on a Sunday without fear. It looks like this. Messy. Complicated. Beautiful. Real.

I am not the same person I was when this story began. I am stronger. I am braver. I am more honest with myself and with others. I know my worth now in a way I never did before. I know that I deserved better than what I got, and I know that the fact that I did not get it says everything about the people who hurt me and nothing about my value as a person. That took me decades to learn. But I learned it.

If you are reading this and you are still in the middle of your own darkness, I want you to know something. You are not alone. You are not broken beyond repair. You are not unworthy of love or safety or peace. What happened to you was not your fault, and it does not define your future. You get to decide what comes next. It will not be easy. It will not be quick. But it is possible. I am living proof that it is possible.

Find your P!NK music. Find the thing that brings you back when the darkness gets too heavy. It might be music. It might be a friend like Nat. It might be your children or your grandchildren. It might be a counsellor, a support group, a book, or a walk in the fresh air. Find the thing that reminds you that you are still here, still breathing, still capable of joy. And hold onto it with both hands.

Set boundaries, even when it hurts. Walk away from people who make you smaller. Stop over-explaining yourself to people who have already decided not to understand you. Choose peace over performance. Choose yourself, even when it feels impossible, especially when it feels impossible.

And know this: healing is not linear. There will be days when you feel like you have made no progress at all, when you feel like you are right back where you started. Those days are part of the process. They do not mean you are failing. They mean you are human. Be patient with yourself. Be kind to yourself. You are doing the best you can with what you have, and that is enough.

I am still standing. After everything, I am still here. I have been knocked down more times than I can count. I have been hurt by people who were supposed to protect me. I have been broken and bruised and left for dead, metaphorically and almost literally. But I got back up. I kept going. I kept fighting. Not because I am special or uniquely strong, but because I refused to let the people who hurt me have the final word on my life. I refused to let my story end in their darkness. I chose to write a different ending. And so can you.

This is my story. It is not pretty. It is not easy to read. But it is true. And it is mine. No one gets to rewrite it. No one gets to tell me it was not that bad, or that I should be over it by now, or that I am dwelling on the past. This is my past, and I get to speak it out loud. I get to name what happened to me. I get to say: this was wrong, and it hurt, and I survived it anyway.

And now I get to live my future on my own terms. I get to choose love. I get to choose safety. I get to choose peace. I get to wake up every morning and decide that today, I will keep going.

Today, I will choose life. Today, I will choose myself. And that is the greatest victory of all.

I am still standing. And if you are reading this, so are you. Keep standing. Keep fighting. Keep choosing yourself. The world needs your story. The world needs your strength. The world needs you, exactly as you are, scars and all. You are worthy. You are loved. You are enough. And you are still standing.

Savannah in The Go-Kart

ZJ's 2nd birthday party, having lunch with Savannah and baby T

Poppy Darren and ZJ On the Go-Kart

Joanne Maree Duggan

ZJ On the Jumping Castle

ZJ and Poppy Darren On the Jumping Castle

Joanne Maree Duggan

Savannah On the Jumping Castle

EPILOGUE

In early February, we celebrated ZJ's second birthday. The Friday night before the party, I was up late in the kitchen while ZJ slept, cooking and getting all the party food ready. I tried to make most of the food in dinosaur shapes because ZJ is going through that phase right now, the way toddlers do when they find something they love and want to see it everywhere. I just wanted everything to be perfect for him. That feeling sits in my chest whenever I plan something for ZJ, this fierce desire to give him joy, to give him moments of pure childhood happiness that are uncomplicated and safe. He deserves that. He deserves so much more than what he has been given.

Saturday morning, I finished the cakes, decorating some with cream and others with icing sugar, carefully placing little dinosaurs on top of each one. Then it was time for me to get changed. I had hired a clown outfit for the day, something I had been looking forward to all week. I painted my face like a clown, taking my time with the colours, and to finish it off, I put on my clown wig. When ZJ saw me, his face lit up in a way that made every bit of effort worth it. He was up and running around, having an absolute ball. We were outside on his jumping castle when the family started to arrive.

Bridgette, my daughter, came with her partner, Jake, and their children: Savannah, baby T, and Nevaeh. It is always hard to get all my grandchildren together at the same time. Some are in high school now, doing their own thing with their friends, living their own lives as they should be. But ZJ did not mind. He had a ball. ZJ and the rest of my grandchildren played on the jumping castle, and they all had a laugh at their nan in the clown outfit. I loved every bit of it, just as much as they did. Watching them play together, hearing their laughter, seeing ZJ so happy and surrounded by family, it filled something in me that I did not even know was empty.

We had lunch, and then our party food, followed by singing happy birthday to ZJ. There was so much love and excitement. It was perfect. Darren also gave the children go-kart rides, and they all loved it. Yes, they all wore protective gear. I made sure of that. Darren's mother, Karen, was also there celebrating with us, and having her there felt right. She has become such an important part of our lives, and I am grateful for her warmth and her acceptance.

Once Bridgette and her family left, I played with ZJ and his cars for a while, just the two of us. Then it was time to take ZJ back to the contact centre, where I dropped him off for his mother, Sammy, to collect him. This is the part of the day I dread. It is hard. It gets harder every time. ZJ does not want to go back. The older he gets, the harder it becomes. He screams and cries when he has to leave me. This is happening more and more, and it breaks my heart seeing him like this. He is so upset, clinging to me, and there is nothing I can do about it. I must follow the court orders, even though every fibre of my being wants to scoop him up and take him home with me. Poor little man does not want to leave me, and at this stage, there is nothing I can do about it.

Sadly, the court orders state I can have ZJ every Friday night from 4:15 PM to Saturday 4:15 PM. That is all. One day a week. One night. It does not feel like enough. It will never feel like enough. But it is what I have, and I hold onto it fiercely.

The next Saturday, Darren, Karen, and I took ZJ to the beach. Personally, I do not like the beach. Never have. But it was a new experience for ZJ, and that was all that mattered. ZJ loved every minute of it. At first, he was unsure about standing in the water with the sand moving under his feet. He would hold onto me tight, his little hands gripping my arms, his eyes wide. But then he was fine. He adjusted, the way children do, finding his balance and his confidence. ZJ and I chased the seagulls together, and he was having a great time. He built sandcastles with Darren, his little hands patting the sand into shape. He would run up and down on the sand, pulling his wagon behind him, laughing that pure, unfiltered laugh that only small children have.

Seeing how much ZJ loved the beach, I will definitely be bringing him back. My own discomfort does not matter. His joy does. Once we got home, ZJ was worn out. I put him down for a nap, and he slept for an hour or so. Then, after his nap, it was time for me to take him back to the contact centre. This part of the day I hate. I hate it with everything in me. I hate seeing him so upset, knowing what is coming, knowing he will cry and cling and beg not to go.

We came up with a plan to make it less traumatic for him. I still drive ZJ to the contact centre, but Darren takes him in. This way, it is not me physically handing him over. So far, that is working. It is a small thing, but it helps. ZJ still cries, but not quite as desperately. And that is something, at least.

I believe ZJ's mother is still on drugs. Sadly, most nights when I get ZJ, he will sleep for eleven to fifteen hours straight. At first, I would wake him up because I thought he was sleeping too much. But I quickly realised he needed it. He was just so worn out. That kind of exhaustion in a small child is not normal. It tells me everything I need to know about what his life is like when he is not with me.

When ZJ is not with me, I get messages from Sammy's and James's friends telling me that Sammy is driving around high on meth with ZJ and his sister in the car, all hours of the night. They tell me she is also selling meth, passing the drugs over in front of the children. Hearing this breaks my heart. Every single time. But I keep doing what I have to do. I keep reporting this to the right people, even when it feels like nothing changes, even when it feels like I am shouting into a void.

ZJ continues to come to me with nappy rash and nappies that are too small for him. He always seems to have a cold. These are the small signs of neglect that add up, that paint a picture I wish I did not have to see. But I do see it. And I document it. And I keep fighting.

Then one Friday morning at 8:30 AM, I received a call from a welfare officer. They told me they had removed ZJ and his sister from Sammy's care and placed them with her mother while they do a three-week assessment on her. This is great news. Sadly, though, I feel that placing them with Sammy's mother is not the answer. She works full-time, and these poor children are still being pulled from pillar to post. I also believe Sammy has five new charges she is going to court for. I believe they are for selling drugs and for driving under the influence of meth. At last, I am happy that welfare is getting involved. At last, they believe me. At last, they can see that Sammy's family has not been honest about what is really going on.

I have gone back to my lawyers. This time, we will be asking the court to return ZJ to my care full-time. I believe this may take some time. The legal system moves slowly, frustratingly slowly, especially when a child's safety is at stake. But I will keep fighting for ZJ. I will be his voice while he cannot speak for himself. I will not give up. I will never give up.

My relationship with Darren is great. It is easy, or at least easier than anything I have ever known. I mean, we all work on our relationships. That is part of it. But Darren is patient with me. We both put the same amount of energy into it. It is not one-sided, which is new to me. There are lots of new things when it comes to Darren, and it is great. I feel so safe with him. All my mental walls have just about disappeared. There are still some there, I would be lying if I said otherwise. But they are coming down, brick by brick, day by day. And that feels like freedom.

My friendship with Nat is still as strong as ever. We text daily or every other day. We catch up on Fridays. His friendship means the world to me. He is the first male who has never judged me or tried to fix me, and I will forever be grateful for that kind of friendship. It is rare to find someone who just accepts you as you are, who does not need you to be anything other than yourself. Nat has been that person for me, and I do not take it for granted.

At this stage in my life, I have stopped seeking my mother's approval. I would not say it is because I do not care anymore. It is because I know now I will never get her approval, no matter how hard I try. And that is okay with me today. So I still keep my distance from her. I do still call her on her birthday, on Mother's Day, and on Christmas Day to wish her well. I do this because it is the right thing for me to do. Not for her. For me. It is about the kind of person I want to be, not about the kind of mother she was or was not.

I have let go of the fantasy that she will one day wake up and see me, really see me, and acknowledge what she put me through. I have let go of the hope that she will apologise, take responsibility, or even admit that things were not okay. She will not. And I have made peace with that. It took me decades, but I have made peace with it. I do not need her validation anymore. I have my own.

This is my life today. It is not perfect. There are still battles to fight, still nights when I lie awake worrying about ZJ, still moments when the old fears creep back in. But it is mine. I have built it from the ruins of what came before. I have chosen safety over chaos. I have chosen love over fear. I have chosen myself, again and again, even when it was hard, especially when it was hard.

I wake up every morning next to a man who loves me without conditions. I have a relationship with Darren's mother that fills a space I did not know was empty. I have my best friend, Nat, who has walked beside me through so much. I have my children and my grandchildren, who are the reason my heart keeps beating. I have P!NK's music, which saved my life more times than I can count. And I have myself. I have reclaimed myself. That is the victory.

The fight for ZJ continues. It will continue for as long as it needs to. I will show up to every court date. I will document everything. I will make every phone call and file every report. I will not stop until he is safe. Until he is home with me, where he belongs. Because that little boy deserves a childhood that is not defined by chaos and drugs and instability, he deserves to sleep because he is tired from playing, not because he is exhausted from surviving. He deserves to know that someone is fighting for him, that someone sees him, that someone will not give up on him no matter what.

I am that someone. I will always be that someone. Because I know what it feels like to be a child who needs protecting and does not get it. I know what it feels like to be scared and alone and convinced that no one cares. I will not let ZJ feel that way. Not if I can help it. Not while I am still breathing.

This is where my story stands today, not at an ending, but at a continuation. Life keeps moving forward. Challenges keep coming. But so do moments of joy. So do moments of peace. So do moments when I look around at the life I have built and think: I did this. I survived. I healed. I kept going. And I am still here.

I am still standing. And I will keep standing, for myself, for ZJ, for every person who has ever felt unlovable or broken or beyond repair. We are not beyond repair. We are not unlovable. We are survivors. And our stories matter. My story matters. And I am proud to tell it.

A NOTE ABOUT MY SON JAMES

I want to share some things about my son James, because through this book I have not really explained what he is like as a person, and he deserves to be seen fully.

James is loving, caring, and has a great sense of humour. I would like to think he gets that from me. James and I have a fantastic mother-son relationship. He knows he can confide in me with anything, and I will listen without judgement. A lot of people today see someone with tattoos and judge them, especially if they have face tattoos as James does. They judge him all wrong. Do not get me wrong, when James has done anything wrong, I am the first to say so. I am not one of those mothers who sugar-coats his wrongdoings. But I am also the first to stand up beside him when he has been blamed for something he has not done.

James has a way of putting a smile on your face whenever he jokes around or just walks into a room. There is a lightness about him that draws people in. Whenever James has been in a room with children, they are drawn to him instantly. James will get down to their level and play with them, giving them his full attention in a way that is rare and beautiful to watch. Whenever I have been sick, James is the first one to rock up at home and move in to take care of me, no matter what is going on in his own life. That is who he is. That is the son I raised.

James does have his own battles with addiction, and he knows it. But the difference between him and Sammy is that James wants to put his children first. He wants to stay clean for them, and he has my full support in that. Sadly, Sammy and her family do not think she has a drug problem, and that is where the difference lies.

Seeing James joke around with his two older daughters, Indii and Jaydah, is beautiful. Seeing him play with ZJ melts my heart. They all adore their father, and he adores them. We do lots of family outings together, like bowling and trips to the park. These are the moments that matter.

James asked me to help with ZJ because he knew Sammy would not do the right thing, and he also knew he could not do it on his own while getting clean. I said yes without hesitation. James has been clean for six months now, and I am so proud of him. Six months might not sound like a long time to some people, but to anyone who has battled addiction, six months is a victory. It is proof that change is possible.

James brings so much joy into our lives, and he deserves to be happy. I love you, boy. You have created a new, clean life for yourself. Enjoy it. We are so proud of you.

James with His Daughter Jaydah

**James and His Daughter Indii Having Toasted
Marshmallows On a Night at Nan's**

James, Indii, Jaydah, and Me

James (daddy) Playing with his Son ZJ

Still Standing